Lighter of Gospel Fires

By
Ella M. Robinson

TEACH Services, Inc.
Brushton, New York

PRINTED IN
THE UNITED STATES OF AMERICA

World rights reserved. This book or any portion thereof may not be copied or reproduced in any form or manner whatever, except as provided by law, without the written permission of the publisher, except by a reviewer who may quote brief passages in a review.

The author assumes full responsibility for the accuracy
of all facts and quotations as cited in this book.

Facsimile Reproduction

As this book played a formative role in the development of Christian thought and the publisher feels that this book, with its candor and depth, still holds significance for the church today. Therefore the publisher has chosen to reproduce this historical classic from an original copy. Frequent variations in the quality of the print are unavoidable due to the condition of the original. Thus the print may look darker or lighter or appear to be missing detail, more in some places than in others.

2007 08 09 10 11 12 · 5 4 3 2 1

Copyright © 2002 TEACH Services, Inc.
ISBN-13: 978-1-57258-224-8
ISBN-10: 1-57258-224-3
Library of Congress Control Number: 2002095368

Published by

TEACH Services, Inc.
www.TEACHServices.com

CONTENTS

1. Boyhood Memories 1
2. The Singing Class 6
3. A Sad Summer 10
4. Confused Thinking 15
5. Grandfather's Stories 19
6. A Long-Remembered Night 24
7. Waiting 30
8. School Days 39
9. Answering the Call 45
10. Facing New Light 55
11. An Evil Spirit Rebuked 65
12. The Silver Three-Cent Piece 74
13. Perplexing Problems 82
14. Across the Prairies 87
15. Public Evangelism Advances 100
16. Brighter Days 111
17. Westward to California 118
18. Efforts to Put Out the Fire 130
19. A Day of Miracles 137
20. The Prospector 146
21. The First Camp Meeting in California . 152
22. Beginnings in Oakland 158
23. Closing Years 165

DEDICATION

This narration is dedicated to our noble army of youth, ambitious for those honors which may be won by earnest, faithful service to God and by a willingness to follow the pathway of self-denying toil that leads to the heights of eternal glory. "They that be wise shall shine as the brightness of the firmament; and they that turn many to righteousness as the stars for ever and ever."

J.N. Loughborough

BOYHOOD MEMORIES

1

IN A portrait of John Loughborough that many of us have seen, his white beard gives him a dignified, patriarchal look. However, it scarcely hides a half-suppressed smile, which seems to invite one to listen as he tells a story of adventurous and self-sacrificing exploits in the early days of the advent movement. He lived at a time when men went forth fearlessly to proclaim the three angels' messages, often traveling from place to place on foot or by borrowed conveyance, not knowing where they were to sleep at night or how they or their families would be fed and clothed. There are some now in their sunset years who had the privilege of following his thrilling reports sent to the *Review,* or they may have read his "Sketches of the Past" in the *Pacific Union Recorder.* There are still a few who remember his verbal recitals of early adventures in faith, which firmly established his confidence in God's leadership of the remnant people.

John Loughborough's life story begins January 26, 1832, almost two years before the stars fell. He was born in Victor, New York, a village on the stage line between Albany and Buffalo. His earliest recollections were of the family gathered for worship before breakfast and after supper in the big kitchen. Mother would hold the baby while father read from the large picture Bible and explained the words so that all could understand. Everyone, including little Johnny and the hired workmen, was expected to listen reverently to the reading and to kneel while father prayed. Heaven was made very real to the children, a place worth every sacrifice and effort to obtain.

John's grandfather had been a soldier in General George Washington's army in the American Revolution. Naturally grandfather Loughborough's stories of the war were of interest to the grandchildren. Grandson John remembered the incident of George Washington's father telling him, "Son, make up your mind that if there are but two men going to heaven, you will be one of them, and live accordingly."

The Christian influence of the Loughborough family extended beyond their own home. Father and grandfather, although not members of the clergy, were both "local preachers" in the Methodist Episcopal Church. Through their leadership a company of believers was established, and a church building was erected, which became a gathering place for other small congregations in the area, especially at the time of quarterly Communion services. The children regularly attended the services with their parents, and the younger generation sat in reverence, listening to the testimonies of the members as they made public confessions in preparation for the Lord's Supper.

Each one who partook of the bread and wine was required to show a ticket from his Bible-class teacher indicating that his life and conduct were blameless. If there had been a known misconduct, such a one was refused a ticket.

One mother was refused acceptance in the service because she wore golden ornaments. Her daughter's name was taken off the church books because she had been seen at a dance.

On cold and windy days mother Loughborough, who was often in delicate health, was unable to take the children to the sanctuary, and the children played church at home. Although his older brother and sister took part, Johnny always did the preaching and praying. But the others, including the baby, would all join in the singing.

The Loughboroughs lived only a few rods from the meetinghouse, and their home became the center for visitors, ministers, church officers, and inquirers. Thus the main themes of conversation heard by the children were religious matters and the service of the church.

In those days schools were not developed as they are today; but sometimes a good private school was available. One such school was conducted in Victor by a Miss Bibbins. Classes were held in a room in the Methodist church. The children learned to read and write, and to recite poems and Bible verses. Johnny was permitted to attend this school with his older brother and sister. Although he started when he was only three years old, he learned many things at this impressionable age that he never forgot.

At one of the programs given by the school, Johnny surprised his mother by standing bravely beside the teacher's desk when his time came to recite. Without prompting he said:

> Were I so tall as to reach the sky,
>   Or grasp the ocean in my span;
> I must be measured by my soul;
>   The mind's the standard of the man.

The applause was immediate. Johnny looked around in a startled way, and then, thinking that the clapping was a regular part of the program, joined in it vigorously, to the amusement of the audience.

Since Johnny was less than two years old on that wonderful night in November, 1833, when the cascade of stars fell from the sky, he could not remember it. Nevertheless he enjoyed hearing his father and mother recount the story on many occasions, declaring it to be one of the signs of the return of Jesus.

The rural environment brought the children many simple pleasures and duties. Driving the family cow a quarter of a mile to pasture every morning and bringing her back in time for milking was fun. The young man who worked on the neighboring farm where Brindle was pastured enjoyed giving Johnny horseback rides round the orchard and through the field.

One morning Johnny lagged behind his brother and sister in order to ride the horse a little longer. Since this caused him to be late for school, his mother warned him he must not do it again.

"Now, John, you must come home with the other children," his mother said the next morning as he started with them to the pasture. "If you come home late you cannot go to the school today, and I shall whip you besides."

Five-year-old Johnny did not mean to disobey, but he yielded to the coaxing of the young man, "Just one little ride." When the other children started home, Johnny wanted to get down off the horse; but the man said, "Oh, your mother won't care; let them go." So Johnny stayed to enjoy the fun a little longer. When he got home he hurried to wash his face and comb his hair; but, as he was starting out the door for school, his mother called, "No, John, you are not going to school today. Then, too, I am going to whip you, as I said I would." All forenoon Johnny had the whipping to think about. He knew it would come sometime, for his mother always meant what she said. They had a good dinner, and everyone seemed happy; nothing was said about John's disobedience. After dinner the boy got ready to go to school with the other children, but his mother said calmly, "No, John, you are not going to school today. I am going to whip you as I told you this morning."

All afternoon Johnny thought about that whipping, yet it did not come. Finally, about five o'clock in the evening, she came into the house with a peach sprout in her hands and tears in her eyes. "Punishing you hurts me more than it hurts you," she said. He cried, but mother cried more than he did. That was the last whipping Johnny ever received.

Like other children, the Loughborough youngsters enjoyed watching trained animals perform their tricks. They lived before the day of great circuses, but there were traveling animal shows, and when the menagerie came to town, father Loughborough took his family to see the animals. The children were delighted with the monkey dressed like a boy, who rode on the back of a pony, performing tricks as he went. There were huge lions in cages, and there was a basket of baby lions. The animal show furnished conversation in the family for days and weeks.

THE SINGING CLASS

~2~

JOHNNY'S father, like his grandfather, was a cabinetmaker and carpenter. He had a large shop where he made furniture to sell, and he usually hired a number of workmen to help him. By the time Johnny was five years old, the little kindergarten class at the church had outgrown the Sunday-school room, and the class was moved to the basement of the Presbyterian church. Joseph Hollister was hired to teach the older children to read and write and work arithmetic problems, while the smaller tots were kept at their play. Johnny did not want to stay behind with the little ones. One day, when the older children were reading their compositions to their class, he handed the teacher his composition to read. The teacher said, "I can't make it out, Johnny; you read it yourself." Johnny stood up and read what he supposed he had written.

It was not until he was seven years old and had mastered the three R's that his teacher handed the old composition to him with a smile. Johnny saw for the first time that what he had supposed he read to the school that day was merely a page of scribbled pencil marks.

Principles of truth and integrity were instilled by oft-repeated rhymes, such as the following:

It is a sin to steal a pin,
Much more to steal a greater thing;
I'll beg my bread from door to door,
Rather than steal my neighbor's store.

Several evenings a week the children met in the schoolroom for a singing class. The teacher had a tuning fork which would give them the correct pitch, and from there they would go up or down the scale until they reached the first note of the song they were about to sing. The fact that the choir leader who led the hymns in church on Sunday morning used a tuning fork added greatly to the enchantment of this little instrument.

A few years later a violin was used in church to start the hymns and to keep the choir on the right tune. Some of the members did not like to see a violin used in the church, because violins were associated with dances; but the minister insisted that the improved singing was more acceptable to God, and that the tunes helped a person remember the words. He showed them from the Bible that it is a good thing to sing praises to God upon the harp and upon other stringed instruments. He read the one-hundred-fiftieth psalm, in which David extols the use of trumpet, psaltery, harp, stringed instruments, and organs, and even high-sounding cymbals.

One day the students in the school were saddened by the death of one of their classmates, a little girl of seven who was greatly loved because of her kind disposition. On the day of her funeral one of the schoolboys gathered the younger children together and gave them a lecture on the soul. He said that it took three days for the soul to get to heaven. Since the little girl had been dead three days, they could be certain she was already in heaven with Jesus.

For days afterward Johnny would go out and look up at the sky, trying to imagine he could see the little girl sitting on the clouds, and hear her singing the songs they all sang in school. He had once heard a minister say that the souls of good people spent their time sitting on clouds and singing hymns.

John Loughborough preserved the following verses as specimens of his teacher's choice of musical selections for concert work in the class:

> If ever I see on bush or tree,
>   Young birds in a pretty nest;
> I'll not in my play steal the birds away,
>   To grieve their mother's breast.

And again:

> Let dogs delight to bark and bite,
>   For God hath made them so;
> Let bears and lions growl and fight,
>   For 'tis their nature to;
> But little children should not let
>   Such angry passions rise;
> Their little hands were never made
>   To tear each other's eyes.

One day Johnny watched his father and uncle lay the foundation of a house. His uncle said, "Johnny, if you will take your little wheelbarrow and move that pile of stones to the side of the fence, you will find a sixpenny piece under the last stone you move." As Johnny put the last stone in the wheelbarrow he saw the sixpence. Proudly he put it into his pocket and began to wonder what would be the best way to spend it.

The next Sunday at church a missionary from Africa gave

a report of the people of that far-off country. He spoke particularly about the children he had been teaching in his mission school. He stated that a sixpence would buy a New Testament in which a child could learn to read the stories of Jesus. Now Johnny knew what he was going to do with his coin. When anyone asked him, he would say, "I am going to send a New Testament to Africa."

A day was set for the church people to bring their gifts of money and clothing to the minister's house for the missionary. On that day Johnny's mother sent him to buy something at the grocery store. The grocer had some special goodies on the counter that he knew Johnny liked. He said, "You may have them all for sixpence, Johnny." The boy's hand went into his pocket, but then he thought of the children in Africa and the New Testament he wanted to send them. He turned and ran out of the store without spending his money.

Johnny hurried to the minister's house, where the church members were gathering. He handed the sixpence to the minister, saying, "Mr. Mapes, here is sixpence; I want to send a Testament to the heathen." Then he quickly ran out of the room. The minister held up the coin, and when the people saw what a five-year-old boy had done, they reached into their pockets and gave more generously.

A SAD SUMMER

3

FATHER LOUGHBOROUGH was working beyond his strength. Besides building houses and making furniture, he was also the only coffinmaker in that part of the country. He held meetings every Sunday with companies of church members scattered several miles from his home. Sometimes he did not return from the meetings until eleven o'clock at night. On arriving it was not uncommon for him to find a rush order for a coffin. Although he had seventeen men working for him in his shop, Mr. Loughborough was the only one who knew how to trim coffins. That meant he had to work the remainder of the night to get the coffin ready.

This summer Mr. Loughborough was so worn out from extra work that when typhoid fever struck him, he had no vitality to resist the disease. When called to treat Mr. Loughborough, the family doctor bled the patient and then dosed him with strong medicine. Although the sick man was hot with fever, he was not allowed to have any water to drink or even a cool sponge bath to reduce the fever. The patient was deprived of fresh air, which was considered dangerous for a sick person. The four-poster bed was cov-

A Sad Summer

ered with heavy drapes, and at one side, near the top of the bed, there was a small opening through which the children were permitted to look at their father.

Under such conditions there was little chance for the patient's recovery. When father Loughborough died at the age of thirty-six, his funeral was one of the largest ever held in the community. Johnny had never seen so many people together before. The church building was crowded, and hundreds of people stood outside. Several ministers helped conduct the funeral services.

In those days little was known about healthful living. On the Loughborough table meat was often served three times a day. For breakfast there was fried pork and rich gravy to cover the bread. At dinnertime the family sat down to boiled pork or corned beef. At supper there was dried beef or ham, with pie or shortcake so rich with lard that Johnny could squeeze the grease out of it with his spoon. There was always plenty of tea or coffee on the table.

In summer when fresh vegetables from the garden were served on the table, these were usually covered with pepper or horse-radish. There were pickles and hard cheese, and sharp cider vinegar to season the salads. In winter, when they had no fresh vegetables, there was an abundance of beans and potatoes as well as rich cakes and pastries.

As a young man John Loughborough learned the harmful effects of the foods he had been accustomed to eating, and he chose the better way of living. He had once been advised by a misguided physician that smoking cigars would benefit his lungs and help him overcome a cough that he had acquired. John learned that tobacco could damage his body, and he discarded the smoking habit.

As he grew older he improved in health and overcame some of the diseases that had afflicted him in youth. He had been deaf in one ear as a result of scarlet fever when he was two years old. While he was recovering from the fever the hired girl had held him in her lap by an open window. A strong breeze had caused congestion in the right ear, which had ulcerated and become permanently deaf. When he was fifty years old, his deaf ear was healed; and for forty years after that he could hear with it as well as with the other.

John was seven years old when his father died. As there were two older and two younger children in the family, the boy was sent to live with his grandfather, who owned a farm three miles from Victor. There the boy found plenty of work doing little tasks and errands for his aunt and helping the hired man with the farm work. The part John liked best was riding the plow horse. From his high seat he could look back and see the steel plow turn furrow after furrow of brown earth. He enjoyed riding the harrow as it smoothed the ground for the planting of the seed.

Haying was a busy season, for the crop was cut with hand scythes. The hay was spread out to dry, and it was turned over several times, until it was thoroughly dry. The wheat was also cut with hand scythes, to which frames called "cradles" were attached. The cradles caught the wheat as it was cut, and laid it out in neat windrows. Then it was gathered with a hand rake, bound into sheaves, and tied with strands of wheat. Johnny helped the men shock the wheat by gathering the sheaves and standing them with their heads up in piles of about a dozen, where they were left to dry in the sun until it was time to gather them in.

A Sad Summer

On the Loughborough farm a crude threshing machine about five feet square was used to thresh the wheat. This threw the straw out at the back, while the wheat and chaff fell on the ground under the machine. Johnny was given the tedious job of shoveling the wheat and chaff out from under the machine. For this shoveling he received twenty-five cents a day. This task had to be done by a boy short enough to permit the straw to pass over his head. Once an hour the threshing operation was stopped long enough for the machinery to be oiled. When this was being done, Johnny could rest while the men shoveled the wheat and chaff into piles.

No person who has lived near a modern wheat ranch, where he has seen the tractors, plows, harrows, planters, and combines at work, can imagine the labor required a hundred years ago when every process was done by hand. The old-fashioned methods did develop strong muscles, and the exercise in the open air helped to counteract some of the effects of the intemperate eating of the time.

In those days there were many Universalists in that part of the country, who ridiculed the doctrine of a judgment day. They believed that God was too merciful to destroy any man, no matter how wicked he might have been. "The Universalists taught a superabundance of free grace, and that the Lord so loved everybody that all were to be saved irrespective of character. Out of this grew a sharp contest between those holding the idea of an endless hell of torment for sinners, and those advocating the idea of sinners dying in their sins and going directly to heaven, thus escaping all further punishment." In opposition to the doctrine held by the Universalists, the Methodists believed in hell-fire and taught it vehemently. Sometimes as the big farm wagon would roll along the road, bringing the family home from church, Johnny would hear shouts of "Old Methodists! Old Methodists!" Once grandfather found several lengths of his fence torn down and stray cattle eating his corn and trampling down his grain. Without saying a word he drove out the cattle and, while the troublesome neighbor and his boys looked on and made sneering remarks, he set up the fence again. Then he went into the house to pray for those who had treated him unkindly.

Another Sunday when the family came home, they noticed that their cherry trees had been stripped of the ripe fruit. Large branches loaded with the cherries had been broken off from the trees. Weeks afterward the dead branches were found in a grove half a mile away. There was a large pear tree on the farm which usually bore four barrels of extra-good pears. Grandfather Loughborough had promised to sell these choice pears to a man who shipped fine fruit to New York City. The man had brought four empty barrels and left them under the tree, ready to be filled on a Monday morning. When the family came home from church on Sunday, not a pear was left on the tree. Months afterward the rotten pears were found under a haystack in the field. Not a word of reproach was spoken by any member of the family, for they had learned to follow the instruction of the Saviour: "Love your enemies, do good to them which hate you, bless them that curse you, and pray for them which despitefully use you."

CONFUSED THINKING

4

EVERY week John's Sunday-school teacher gave the class a portion of Scripture to memorize and repeat as part of their next lesson. One Sunday the class was given the Ten Commandments to memorize. John spent all that afternoon committing the verses in Exodus 20 to memory, and by Monday morning he could repeat them all correctly.

That morning the teacher of the day school planned a concert exercise for the pupils—they were to name the days of the week. She began: "Sunday, first day; Monday, second day." When she had reached that point she stopped speaking and looked up in surprise. Someone was not following the teacher, and it caused confusion. While most of the pupils were saying, "Sunday, first day; Monday, second day," someone was saying, "Monday, first day; Tuesday, second day." One boy was thinking about the Ten Commandments he had learned to repeat the afternoon before. He supposed, of course, that the seventh day which they were commanded to keep holy was Sunday, the day on which they went to Sunday school and the day when he was forbidden to play games. If Sunday was the seventh day, Monday must be the first day. How could he honestly say it was the second day?

The teacher started the exercise again. But again the same voice kept saying, "Monday, first day; Tuesday, second day."

"Who is saying, 'Monday, first day'?" she demanded. No one stirred or made a sound until the courageous dissenter raised his hand.

"You say it as I do, John, or I'll give you a whipping," the teacher announced in a decided voice. John did not like whippings, and the threat frightened him into submission. So he followed the teacher, under protest. Perhaps she does not know the fourth commandment, and so has the days mixed up, he thought.

As soon as he reached home that afternoon, he went at once to his aunt and told her what the teacher had said.

"Teacher is right," she replied. "Sunday is the first day of the week. You had better say it as the rest do."

"But, auntie, the fourth commandment in my Sunday-school lesson said that we should keep the seventh day holy because it is the Sabbath of the Lord. Is Saturday the Sabbath?"

The question seemed to bother her for a minute. Then she answered, "Saturday used to be the Sabbath, but Christ changed it to Sunday." John thought that his aunt must know what she was talking about, so he dropped the question.

Years afterward he had one of his cousins write to his aunt and ask her to tell him where he could find the scripture stating that Jesus had changed the Sabbath from Saturday, the seventh day, to Sunday, the first day. Of course she could not find any text to support the popular idea that Jesus and His disciples changed the Sabbath day appointed at creation. She sent word back to him, "Tell John that I had rather he would keep the seventh day than not to keep any day at all."

John could not find any place in the Bible where Jesus called Sunday the Lord's day. He did find a text which says that He declared Himself to be the Lord of the Sabbath, and he reasoned that if Jesus is Lord of the Sabbath, then the Sabbath must be the Lord's day. When he read church history he learned that the Christians who lived in the early centuries gradually accepted the pagan Sunday instead of Saturday as the day of rest.

As he studied the prophecies of the Bible he learned that before Jesus Christ will return to this earth many people would return to "the old paths." They would show their love and loyalty to God *by keeping all His commandments.* Young Loughborough began to see the great controversy that was behind the attempt to change God's holy Sabbath day.

As John grew older, he studied deeper into the Bible truths concerning man's salvation, and he determined that if he were ever tempted to break one of the Ten Commandments he would remember the promise: "Blessed are they that do His commandments, that they may have right to the tree of life, and may enter in through the gates into the city."

As John became more useful as a farm hand, his grandfather allowed him a small monthly wage for his services. The boy enjoyed reading, and he wanted to have a paper of his own coming to him through the mail; therefore he sent fifty cents for a year's subscription to the *Sunday School Advocate*.

About this time he determined to read his Bible through.

When he came to the story of Eve eating the forbidden fruit he said quite decidedly, "If I had been there in the Garden of Eden, and if I had been Eve and had known that God said not to eat the fruit, I would have let it alone."

One issue of the *Advocate* contained a picture that made an indelible impression on John's mind. In later years he described it in these words:

"The illustration was entitled, 'A picture for all those who play at games of chance.' There were four steps rising one above another. On the ground by the side of the first step were two boys playing marbles at the game called 'keeps,' that is, each boy kept as his own all the marbles he knocked out of the ring of marbles laid by the other boy. Each one was laying the captured marbles by his side as his own.

"On the first step was a table, and by it were two young men playing cards, and each one was piling on the table by his side the cards captured in the game. On the next step were two men also playing cards, but by their side on the table were little piles of money—they were gambling. On the third step were also two men at a table with cards. The cards were in their hands, a pile of money was by the side of one man, and the other was in the act of shooting him with a pistol. On the highest step was a hangman's scaffold, and there, hanging in the air from the gibbet was the man who had shot his fellow gambler."

The picture so impressed John that he never played cards or indulged in any form of gambling. In later years he found that one of his boyhood friends, who was tempted to gamble, had been lured into the vice and when desperately in need of money had stolen large sums. Finally, the trapped man ended his life by taking poison.

GRANDFATHER'S STORIES

∽5∾

GRANDFATHER LOUGHBOROUGH had a headful of interesting stories about his boyhood that young John enjoyed hearing. There was the dramatic moment when Robert Fulton launched his first steamboat, the "Clermont." It made a voyage of one hundred fifty-four miles up the Hudson River from New York to Albany in thirty-two hours. It was a matter of public knowledge that Mr. Fulton had been making a boat to be propelled by a steam engine; but almost everyone said it would never run. Thousands of persons were watching from the riverbank as the boat chugged from the pier. Soon it came to a halt, and the crowds shouted and laughed in derision. But Mr. Fulton knew what the trouble was. Since he had no safety valve on the engine he had used a plug instead. The plug had blown out, leaving the engine without steam. He waved to the crowds and shouted that the trouble would be repaired in a minute. He put the plug in place, fastened it more firmly, fired up the boiler, and the "Clermont" steamed up the river. Then the people cheered loudly. As grandfather told the story, John would always shout, "Three cheers for Fulton!"

As the small boat made its way up the river, with smoke rolling from its smokestack and the paddle wheels churning the water into white foam, one man became frightened. He ran off, crying at the top of his voice, "Hell has broken loose, and the devil is running away with a sawmill." Another man who lived some distance from the river heard the shrieking of the whistle, and thought it was a panther screaming. He gathered his neighbors to help hunt the animal.

Before John was ten years old, the railroad from Rochester to Albany was completed. The track was made by laying down crossties and fastening long strips of timber to them. Iron strips were then attached to the timbers. The cars were twenty feet long, with ceilings so low there was barely room for a man to stand. The engine chugged along, throwing out sparks that endangered the passengers' clothing. There was little danger of collisions in those days, for the trains moved so slowly that an engineer had plenty of time to stop the cars if he saw a train coming from the opposite direction. It required two hours and a half to make the seventeen-mile run from Victor to Rochester—a little faster than a trotting horse could travel.

John remembered the astonishment of the people when they first heard of telegrams. A minister visiting his grandfather said, "They have a way now that they can send letters by electricity on a wire attached to poles." The two old men tried to solve the problem as to how the letters could get around the poles. A few days later the same minister said, "I have learned that they do not send letters written on paper, but they make the electricity spell out the words."

John would listen intently while his grandfather told about the dark day of May 19, 1780. That day grandfather had been working with another young man, shingling the roof of a large two-story house in Perth Amboy, New Jersey. By eleven o'clock it had become so dark that neither of them could see the mark made by their chalk line. After pounding their fingers several times in the darkness, they decided to stop work. They found the housewife lighting kerosene lamps. There was the utmost confusion everywhere, for some persons were crying, and some were confessing sins and calling on God for mercy. The general opinion was that the judgment day had come. The lighted parlor lamp looked like a dim, blue globe and could be seen only a few feet away. Grandfather said that it was as dark as midnight until eleven o'clock that night. Then a glimpse of the moon could be seen. It gave little light, but looked like a ball of blood. Grandfather Loughborough considered the event to be an exact fulfillment of the prophecy of Joel, which says, "The sun shall be turned into darkness, and the moon into blood, before the great and the terrible day of the Lord come."

After this dramatic event, and the falling of the stars on November 13, 1833, grandfather always said, as he made his plans, "I will do this if the Lord does not come."

The summer following John's tenth birthday he was impressed by a tragic incident. A neighbor, who lived about a mile from grandfather Loughborough's farm, was sitting at the dinner table in his home, finishing a hearty meal, when he suddenly collapsed and died of a heart attack. John wanted to go to the funeral, but he could not be spared from the farm work. The ten-acre cornfield had been cultivated, and the rows of corn must be hoed before the rains came. The lad knew nothing about heart disease and supposed that he was in as great danger of dropping dead as was the elderly neighbor. John went about his task in a sober mood, more determined than ever to do his work faithfully so that if he should die he would be taken to heaven.

On one side the cornfield was bordered by woods. John hoed the first row of corn until he came to the grove of trees. He knelt by the fence and prayed earnestly that God would forgive his sins. He hoed the next row of corn to the other side of the patch, and then the third row back to the woods. Every time he came to the fence by the grove of trees he knelt and prayed. The boy longed to be a Christian, but he did not know how. He had read a Methodist catechism written for children, and he found much helpful instruction.

A few days after the hoeing was finished, the rains came. While they lasted, John worked with his grandfather in the carpenter shop. The boy was still thinking about the man who died suddenly. Grandfather, who was working at the other end of the bench, said, "John, you ought to be a good boy and pray to God every night. If you are not a good boy, when you die God will send you to hell and burn you there through eternity." The boy was stunned. He gripped his tools and stood shuddering with horror. He thought to himself, "I pray every night for the Lord to help me, but what use is it if I have to go to hell after all? God hates me; and if He hates me, how can I expect Him to help me be a good boy?"

For a long time afterward John was so discouraged he almost feared to pray. An uncle, Miles Carter, who was spending a few days in the home, watched John make some candle-lighting matches by dipping little whittled sticks into melted brimstone. The man asked, "John, do you know how hot brimstone is?"

"No, Uncle Miles, I don't know how hot it is."

"I'll tell you how hot it is," the uncle continued. "If you will set your brimstone on fire, take a nailrod [a thin strip of iron blacksmiths used in making horseshoe nails] and hold the end of it in the blaze, the iron will soon begin to melt, and drops will fall into the flame. Hell is a thousand times hotter than that." Then the uncle turned and walked away, leaving John shuddering at the thought.

John lived in fear for several years, until a friend handed him a booklet written by Pastor George Storrs. This message from the Bible showed that people do not go to heaven or to hell when they die; they sleep in their graves until Jesus comes.

"Can it really be true?" John asked himself, as he read every sentence over and over and marked the texts in his Bible. A love for God took the place of the terror he had felt. "God loves me; He will help me to live the Christian life," the youth said with assurance.

Later, when he became a minister, he preached on the subject of "The Natural Mortality of Man." In the audience, listening to every word he spoke, was the uncle who, seven years before, had terrified the young man with the picture of an ever-burning hell.

A LONG-REMEMBERED NIGHT

6

IT WAS the last week in December, 1843, when, with other members of the family, John went to hear the sermons of an Adventist preacher. James Barry was holding a series of meetings at the Methodist church in Victor. John remembered that delightful sleigh ride—the crisp air against his cheek, the glistening snow that crunched and crackled under the sleigh runners, and the jingle of bells that kept time with the trot, trot of the old mare. He remembered, too, the jesting remark about the coming of the Lord made by a neighbor lad, and grandfather's sobering rebuke: "Young man, you had better be careful how you treat this subject before you know what it is."

When the family reached the church, it was crowded. People were standing in the aisles and sitting on the gallery steps. A gentleman invited John to climb up behind him and perch on the back of the bench.

The Methodist pastor was sitting on the rostrum beside Evangelist Barry. Above and back of the pulpit there was a chart illustrating the prophecies of Daniel and the Revelation.

The family was scarcely seated when they heard a rich

A Long-Remembered Night 25

voice from one corner of the church auditorium, and, as a solist sang, he was answered by another clear and melodious voice:

> Hail you! and where do you come from?
>
> I am come from the land of Egypt.
>
> Hail you! and where are you bound for?
>
> I am bound for the land of Canaan.
>
> O Canaan, bright Canaan,
> I am bound for the land of Canaan;
> O Canaan, it is my happy home,
> I am bound for the land of Canaan.

John never forgot that song, and he never forgot the sermon preached that night. The minister read the text: "Fear God, and give glory to Him; for the hour of His judgment is come." He showed from the prophecies of Daniel that the time of the judgment was at hand, and the audience was made to feel that it was standing before the judgment seat of God. The preacher also read Daniel 8:14: "Unto two thousand and three hundred days; then shall the sanctuary be cleansed."

As the people came out of the church that night, they saw a strange and wonderful sight. Stretched across the heavens from southwest to northeast was a band of light that appeared about as wide as the moon's disk. They stood quietly looking at it for a long time. Many were thinking of the prophecy in Joel: "And I will show wonders in the heavens and in the earth, blood, and fire, and pillars of smoke. The sun shall be turned into darkness, and the moon into blood, before the great and the terrible day of the Lord come."

The young man who that evening on his way to meeting

had made fun of the advent teachings now stood looking with awe into the sky. In a trembling voice, he said, "Uncle Nathan, you and the Adventist preachers are right. This is a sign that Jesus is coming soon."

Between 1833 and 1844, while the advent message was being proclaimed in all parts of the world, grand sights in the sky were often seen. They reminded men and women of Christ's prophetic words and made them more willing to listen to the judgment message.

The Adventist minister continued his lectures on the second coming in the Methodist church at Victor, and the Loughborough family went to hear him every night. The solemn messages impressed the hearts of the hearers, and even some of those who came because of curiosity or with intent to ridicule became strangely serious. After the sermon began, scarcely a whisper could be heard in the audience.

As the speaker presented God's love in the plan of salvation, the audience seemed to see Jesus on the cross, bearing the shame and sorrow of their sins. They saw Him standing with outstretched arms, calling them to come to Him, to lay down their burdens and find rest. They saw Him coming in the clouds of heaven in majesty and glory, attended by all the angels. They saw sinners trying to hide from His presence, crying in terror for the rocks and mountains to fall on them and hide them from the wrath of the Lamb. They saw another company looking up with joyful faces, and heard their triumphal shout: "This is our God; we have waited for Him, and He will save us: this is the Lord; we have waited for Him, we will be glad and rejoice in His salvation."

Each service ended with an appeal by the Methodist

pastor, calling sinners to come forward for special prayer. One evening, after a severe struggle, John joined those who were pressing to the front. One of the church members said to him, "So you've decided to be a good boy; I'm glad of it." The youth longed for someone to teach him *how* to be a Christian. A young friend, noticing the tears in John's eyes, whispered, "Trust Jesus. Believe that He forgives your sins, as He has promised to do. Be thankful and happy that He has received you as His child." These words made the entrance to the Christian pathway plain for the youthful inquirer.

When the series of meetings in Victor were finished, Evangelist Barry went to other cities to give the message. Many of the church members continued to gather in small groups to pray for one another and for the unconverted. As the believers became better acquainted with Jesus, their love for one another grew stronger. Words that had injured others were confessed and forgiven, hard feelings were banished, quarrels were settled, and debts were paid. There was little talk about gaining property or wealth; interest in earthly things seemed to die out. Many sold their precious possessions and gave the money to the Adventist preachers to help pay their expenses while traveling from place to place. Some purchased papers and pamphlets to distribute to those who would read. John's grandfather subscribed to two of the advent periodicals, *The Signs of the Times* and *The Midnight Cry*. It was one of John's duties to carry these papers to the neighbors, and, when one family had read them, he picked them up and took them to others.

A young man of sixteen, who was a student in the Sunday school and the day school that John attended, made it a practice to take a group of young boys out into the woods at the noon hour, where they prayed and talked about the Christian life. He did much to help John understand how to be a victorious Christian.

In 1838 Josiah Litch had published a tract in which he showed that if Bible students were correct in believing that a day in prophecy stood for a year of actual time, then the prophecy of Revelation 9 about the Turkish Empire would be fulfilled on August 11, 1840, and Turkey would then lose its power as an independent nation. Many Christians, including the Loughborough family, waited to see if the prophecy would come true. *And it did.* In the exact month of the specific year, four nations of Europe intervened to settle a quarrel between Turkey and Egypt.

Infidels who had ridiculed the idea of the inspiration of the Bible read Litch's tract. When they saw the prophecy fulfilled exactly at the time foretold, they acknowledged that the Bible prophecies were true.

Of this event, John Loughborough wrote in later years, "This day (August 11th) the period of three hundred and ninety-one years and fifteen days allotted to the continuance of the Ottoman power ended; and where was the sultan's independence? Gone! . . . The accurate fulfillment of the prophecy gave an impetus to the advent proclamation such as it had never before received. Dr. Litch ascertained that not less than one thousand infidels renounced their infidelity and accepted the Bible on witnessing the fall of the Ottoman supremacy, as set forth in the accurate fulfillment of the prophecy."

The Loughboroughs and their fellow believers were thrilled as they read reports of the progress the advent

A Long-Remembered Night 29

teaching was making in the world. Three hundred ministers in the United States alone were giving all their time to preaching the first angel's message: "Fear God, and give glory to Him; for the hour of His judgment is come: and worship Him that made heaven, and earth, and the sea, and the fountains of waters."

As early as 1821 a missionary named Joseph Wolff began preaching the second advent in Ireland, Scotland, and Holland. He also traveled in Asia, Africa, and Europe, spending most of his time in the countries bordering on the Mediterranean Sea.

In some countries men were whipped and put into prison for teaching the advent doctrines. In Sweden it was against the law for anyone to teach any doctrine except the state religion. Here God used children to give the message. One time, after John had become a minister, he preached to many of the Swedish people in Indiana, who had heard children preach the advent message in 1843. Loughborough recounts the story one of the members told him:

"One day I took my four-year-old son and went to a private home where meetings were being held. Quite a company of people had gathered at the house. When I entered, they were singing a Lutheran hymn. Soon the Spirit of the Lord came upon a little girl about four years old. She was lifted by her father and stood upon the table, where she preached a sermon about the coming of Jesus and the judgment. Although not able to read a word, she repeated scripture after scripture, and spoke so earnestly that many sought God with tears. After she had finished speaking she played around like any other little girl until the people came together again."

WAITING

~7~

GRANDFATHER LOUGHBOROUGH, in company with the other believers in Victor, waited patiently for the spring of 1844, the time of expectation. But March passed, then April, and still they waited. Many of the ministers who, at first, had invited the Adventist preachers to lecture in their churches, now closed their doors against them. One day John was surprised and puzzled to hear his Methodist pastor begin the sermon by saying, "I have a confession to make; I wish to say that I am sorry I ever invited the Adventists to preach in this house." The man went on to say that it was a mistake to believe that Christ was coming soon.

"How *can* he be sorry?" John said to himself. "Is he sorry that hundreds of new members were added to his church? Sorry that the saloon in town has been closed? Sorry that infidels were converted? Sorry that one of the worst ruffians in town, who used to get half drunk and then ride his pony through the streets singing rude songs and cursing God, is now telling everybody what the grace of God can do for vile sinners?"

There were many ministers in other churches who had

Waiting 31

witnessed the power of the Holy Spirit and who stood out boldly against the sudden change in public opinion. They refused to give up their hope, and they encouraged their congregations to wait patiently until God should make everything plain.

About this time the Loughboroughs heard strange tidings from Rochester, New York. At the same time that William Miller was holding meetings in a hall in that city, encouraging the advent believers to hold fast their faith and wait patiently for the coming Saviour, one of the leading ministers announced an oyster supper in his church. He also advertised a pamphlet which he had written against the "Millerites."

Those who held firmly to the advent hope were grieved as they saw so many of their friends turn against the solemn message. They were cheered in those trying days by the promise found in Habakkuk 2:2, 3: "Write the vision, and make it plain upon tables, that he may run that readeth it. For the vision is yet for an appointed time, but at the end it shall speak, and not lie: though it tarry, wait for it; because it will surely come, it will not tarry."

The Adventist preachers went forward with their message, explaining the prophecies and helping people prepare to meet Jesus. When churches were closed to them, they hired halls, pitched large tents, or erected tabernacles. They held meetings in schoolhouses, private homes, barns, sheds, and in the groves and meadows. One evangelistic company had a big tent which seated four thousand persons.

After the Methodist minister at Victor had denounced the Adventists, there were members in his church who looked annoyed if a person sang an advent hymn or mentioned the

Lord's soon coming. One Sunday the pastor announced that there would be a church trial of those who persisted in spreading the advent doctrines. The accused members demanded that they be tried by the Bible standard. After the pastor had spent one forenoon attempting to prove from the Bible that they were wrong, he gave up and announced that there would be another session in the afternoon, and the members would be tried by the Methodist discipline. During the noon hour, twenty-one of the members on trial met together and appointed a leader to speak for them. When the meeting was called to order, their spokesman arose and said, "If this is the mode of your procedure, we withdraw from your fellowship. You can take our names off your church records."

Grandfather Loughborough was sad to break with the church he had helped to build up and where he had served as class leader and deacon for many years. The advent believers quietly withdrew and met in small groups in private homes.

While this separation was going on at Victor, similar church trials were being held in many churches in other places. Thousands of earnest members were cast out of their churches because they could not refrain from speaking of "the blessed hope." They found comfort in the promise: "Hear the word of the Lord, ye that tremble at His word; Your brethren that hated you, that cast you out for My name's sake, said, Let the Lord be glorified: but He shall appear to your joy, and they shall be ashamed." Isaiah 66:5.

By the time John was twelve he was doing a man's work on the farm. He was also becoming a good Bible student. In the summertime he did not have much time for study, for the farm work was never finished. When the sun went down, there were always some jobs that had to be left over until the next day. But the precious minutes between sunset and the time to drop wearily into bed were spent studying the Bible and reading the advent papers, with the ever-present question in mind: "How long must we wait for our Lord's return?" The papers were full of hope and courage. They contained letters from various ministers reminding the readers that the prophecy spoke of a tarrying time. They referred to the parable of the ten virgins, where Jesus said "the bridegroom tarried." "We are like the virgins," they said, "waiting for our Lord to return from the wedding."

In the mail one day the family received a copy of *The Second Advent of Christ*, a periodical published by Charles Fitch. It contained an article entitled, "Come Out of Her, My People," calling attention to the fact that a second angel was to follow the first, with the message, "Babylon is fallen, is fallen, that great city, because she made all nations drink of the wine of the wrath of her fornication." He explained that Babylon, in the figurative language of the book of Revelation, represented the churches of Christendom, which were becoming more and more world-loving. The wine of Babylon represented the false doctrines of the churches, by which many ministers were blinding the eyes of the people to important Bible teachings about the coming of Jesus and the judgment.

At the top of the page was this note: "Please read and circulate." Many Adventists were wondering whether they should leave their churches. When they read this article, thousands of sincere believers withdrew their membership and formed separate groups. The message was going into every town and city in the United States. Large halls were rented, and camp meetings were held.

One of the Adventist preachers named Samuel Snow had been teaching for some months that the twenty-three hundred years of the prophecy of Daniel would not end until the fall of the year, instead of in the spring, as was first believed. A five-day camp meeting was held near Exeter, New Hampshire, August 12-17, 1844. This was a long way from Victor, New York, where the Loughboroughs lived, so they could not attend. From the advent periodicals, however, they learned that three thousand persons were on the grounds. Family tents were pitched in the grove; a speaker's platform was erected under the trees, and rows and rows of plank seats were arranged in front of it. The following account was related to John Loughborough many years later.

One day Joseph Bates, an old sea captain, was speaking. He was describing the joy of passengers and sailors on shipboard as their vessel neared the harbor after a long sea voyage. He was encouraging the people to rejoice at the thought that they would soon be at the end of their journey, safe at home with their Redeemer. During the meeting Samuel Snow arrived at the campground on horseback. He hastily cared for his horse and then, with Bible in hand, came into the meeting, and sat down beside Elder and Mrs. John Couch. He held a short whispered conversation with his friends. Suddenly Mrs. Couch beckoned to the speaker.

"What is it, sister?" Joseph Bates asked.

"What you are saying is good," the woman declared: "but here is a man who has something new to tell us; he has light on 'the midnight cry.' "

"Then let him come up here on the platform and give it

to the people," said Bates; and he sat down. The new arrival ascended the platform and addressed the congregation:

"Where are we in the advent experience? Where have we been since April?"

They answered, "We have been in the tarrying time."

"Yes, and we have been asleep, like the ten virgins in the parable. How long did the bridegroom tarry?"

"Till midnight."

"That is right. Tell me, what does a day stand for in prophecy?"

"A day stands for a year."

"Then what would a night be?"

"Half a year, or six months."

"Then is it not plain, that midnight would come in the middle of the six months? We have been in the tarrying time of the message more than three months. We have passed the midnight of the time. I am here to give you 'the midnight cry,' 'Behold, the Bridegroom cometh; go ye out to meet Him.' We are in the tarrying time because we made a mistake in our reckoning. The decree to rebuild Jerusalem that marked the beginning of the 2300-year period did not go forth at the beginning of the year 457 B.C., but in the latter part of it. Therefore the 2300 years should end in the fall of 1844, and not in the spring of that year, as we have supposed."

The people were then reminded that Jesus was crucified on the day of the Passover—the type pointing forward to the true Passover Lamb, who was sacrificed for us. Three days after the Passover, the first sheaf of ripened grain was offered to the Lord. It was called the "wave sheaf," or "sheaf of first fruits," because it represented Jesus, the first fruits of the righteous who will be raised from the dead at His coming. It was on this day of first fruits that Jesus came forth from the grave. Also it was on the Day of Pentecost that the Holy Spirit was poured out upon the disciples.

"Why, then," asked the speaker, "may we not expect that the sanctuary will be cleansed on the tenth day of the seventh month, the day when the cleansing of the sanctuary took place in the wilderness tabernacle and later in the temple at Jerusalem? When does the tenth day of the seventh month of the Jewish year come? This year, 1844, it falls on October 22. May we not look for our Saviour to come and cleanse His sanctuary on that day, and thus complete the fulfillment of the types on the same day of the year on which they were observed in the ceremonial services?"

The power of the Spirit attended the speaker as he solemnly announced, "It is time for us to wake up and give 'the midnight cry,' 'Behold, the Bridegroom cometh; go ye out to meet Him.' " The service ended in a testimony meeting of song, prayer, and praise.

The leaders begged Snow to stay longer and help with the meetings; but he answered, "No, you have the message. I must go on tonight and give it to others." He mounted his horse and galloped off at full speed. But he left the Adventist believers with the definite hope of seeing Jesus October 22, less than three months from that day.

This view of the time prophecy had been suggested by William Miller and others; but it now became a settled conviction with the Adventists. As the time approached, "the midnight cry" swelled to a grand chorus of voices. Everyone prayed, "Come, Lord Jesus; come quickly." As friend met friend in home, street, or shop, the common greeting was,

Waiting

"Jesus is coming; are you ready to meet Him?" or, "Behold, the Bridegroom cometh; is your lamp trimmed and burning?" or, "He will come, and will not tarry."

John Loughborough was happier than he had ever been, for he was trusting in his Saviour and awaiting a home in His heavenly kingdom. Every night, before closing his eyes in sleep, he reviewed the events of the day to see if he had done or said anything that would grieve his Saviour. Not a sin could be left unconfessed until morning. He joined a group of earnest youth who met regularly to pray for the unconverted.

Joyfully the Adventist group approached the day of expectation; but October 22 passed, and Jesus did not come. John was bitterly disappointed. The neighbor boys with whom he had talked about the coming of Jesus now taunted him, "Haven't gone up yet, have you, John?"

Through the sad days that followed, the little company of believers at Victor, as well as hundreds of other Adventist groups in other towns and cities, reviewed the prophecies, trying to find some possible error in their reckoning of the time; but they could not find it. They continued to study and pray, and to wait for the Lord to show them where they had made a mistake.

Of this heartbreaking experience James White wrote, "The disappointment at the passing of the time was a bitter one. True believers had given up all for Christ, and had shared His presence as never before. They had, as they supposed, given their last warning to the world, and had separated themselves, more or less, from the unbelieving, scoffing multitude. . . . The love of Jesus filled every soul, and beamed from every face, and with inexpressible desires they prayed, 'Come Lord Jesus, and come quickly.' But He did not come. And now to turn again to the cares, perplexities, and dangers of life, in full view of the jeers and revilings of unbelievers who now scoffed as never before, was a terrible trial of faith and patience. When Elder Himes visited Portland, Maine, a few days after the passing of the time, and stated that the brethren should prepare for another cold winter, my feelings were almost uncontrollable. I left the place of meeting and wept like a child.

"But God did not forsake His people. His Spirit upon them still abode, with all who did not rashly deny and denounce the good work in the advent movement up to that time. And with especial force and comfort did such passages as the following, to the Hebrews, come home to the minds and hearts of the tried, waiting ones: 'Cast not away therefore your confidence, which hath great recompense of reward. For ye have need of patience, that, after ye have done the will of God, ye might receive the promise. For yet a little while, and He that shall come will come, and will not tarry.'"—*Life Sketches*, 1888 ed., pp. 107, 108.

SCHOOL DAYS

8

"WE SHALL still be receiving our advent papers," said grandfather Loughborough as he brought in the mail one day after a trip to the post office in Victor. *The Signs of the Times,* which had been a friend and guide to the Adventists for many months, was now called the *Advent Herald.* In the November issue of the *Advent Herald* which grandfather brought home that afternoon he read the announcement: "We find that our time has passed, and we are still on the shores of mortality. That we may occupy till the Lord come, we shall continue to furnish our readers with the *Herald,* the little time it may be needed."

So the *Herald* continued to arrive in the mail, sometimes once a week, sometimes once in two weeks, sometimes not so often. But always it brought a comforting and cheering message to the disappointed and waiting ones. Neither the editor nor the contributors seemed to be discouraged. God had blessed the Adventist preaching, they said; sinners had been converted; the word of God had been studied with new interest; God had done a wonderful work on the hearts of the people. Now He was testing them, preparing them for some great event that would soon take place. They must not become discouraged and turn back. Let all remain humble at the foot of the cross until God should make things plain. "Let us look for Him daily until He shall appear," they urged; "then we shall appear with Him in glory."

To reassure the brethren that they had not been deceived by a merely human or fanatical movement, George Storrs printed a letter in *The Midnight Cry,* of October 31, 1844, from which we quote: "At first the definite time was generally opposed; but there seemed to be an irresistible power attending its proclamation, which prostrated all before it. It swept over the land with the velocity of a tornado, and it reached hearts in different and distant places almost simultaneously, and in a manner which can be accounted for only on the supposition that God was in it. It produced everywhere the most deep searching of heart and humiliation of soul before High Heaven. It caused a weaning of affections from the things of this world, a healing of controversies and animosities, a confession of wrongs, a breaking down before God, and penitent, brokenhearted supplications to Him for pardon and acceptance. It caused self-abasement and prostration of soul, such as we have never before witnessed."

In one issue of the *Advent Herald* there appeared a letter from William Miller. He wrote that his faith was stronger than ever. Although disappointed, he was resigned to the will of God. "Now, brethren," he said, " 'ye have need of patience, that, after ye have done the will of God, ye might receive the promise.' "

There were many other letters from Adventist ministers. One letter from a minister in Maine reminded the readers that the message was, "The hour of His judgment is come." There must be a judgment before the advent of Jesus Christ. He believed they were in the hour of the judgment, and that it might require a little period of time for this to take place.

Several of the contributors sounded a warning not to be shaken by the taunts of scoffers. Were not these godless men saying exactly what the Scriptures foretold as they asked, "Where is the promise of His coming?" The believers were cautioned not to be among those who would complain, "The days are prolonged, and every vision faileth." God's promises would not fail.

Let those who would, say it was all a delusion! Was Jonah a false prophet when he proclaimed that Nineveh would be destroyed in forty days? Even though the people of Nineveh repented, and God spared the city, Jonah had preached the message God had given him. The Lord had a purpose in sending the message to the inhabitants of that great city.

Another letter reminded the readers that God told Abraham to offer up his son Isaac, but the faithful man did not have to do it, for God provided another offering instead. Did that prove Abraham to be deluded when he made the journey to Mount Moriah at God's command? No, indeed! The Lord was testing him. Now, the letter went on, God is testing the advent people, to discover those who love Him enough to bear ridicule and to wait patiently for His coming.

"Yes, we know the Lord will come," said grandfather Loughborough, smiling through his tears. "Didn't I see the sun and moon darkened? Didn't I see the stars fall? And I saw all those strange sights in the heavens that were given as signs. Best of all, we have God's promises that never fail."

The *Advent Herald* of January 22, 1845, printed this hymn:

> Hark! hark! hear the blest tidings,
> Soon, soon, Jesus will come,
> Robed, robed in honor and glory,
> To gather His ransomed ones home.

The family sang it together, and it cheered their hearts. Advent songs continued to be sung throughout the land; and they helped bolster the courage of the waiting ones.

Grandfather decided that John should go on with his schooling that winter. He reasoned that the boy ought to get a good education, which would enable him to serve the Lord intelligently as long as time should last. "The Master bids us, 'Occupy till I come,'" grandfather said. "That means that while we wait for His appearing, we should go on with our regular work, being good farmers, or mechanics, or students, being good neighbors, and doing everything we do so faithfully that we shall honor God."

The country school was now a mile from grandfather Loughborough's home, but John did not mind. He was determined to learn all he could from books. He was also fond of mechanics and liked to work with tools. His cousin, who was attending the same school, had a violin. John wanted one like it, but not having money with which to purchase one, he made a violin himself, shaping it from a slab of beech wood. He finished it like the violins sold in the stores, and after deciding that music was not his most productive talent, sold it to a physician. However, John does not tell us what was paid him.

He tried to make everything he could that was described in his physics book entitled, *Comstock's Philosophy.* John tells us, "I constructed an electrical machine, with its glass cylinder for generating the electricity, the Leyden jar with thunder tongs, insulating stools, dancing jacks, hair-raising images, and other paraphernalia." He constructed a galvanic battery of copper and zinc, with a rasp electric coil for administering electric shocks. With this outfit he earned a little money treating a paralytic patient.

Soon his teachers and schoolmates began calling John "the philosopher." At the closing school exercises, when the neighborhood families came together, the young man was called upon to exhibit his electrical machines and to give a lecture on electricity. He was so interested in his subject and in his various machines that he forgot his natural timidity.

In April, 1847, when John was fifteen years old, he went to live with his eldest brother, who had a carriage-maker's shop in Victor. He intended to work in the shop during the summer and attend high school in the winter. But at the end of seven months his brother closed his shop and went to work with another carriage maker in Adam's Basin, a town thirty miles away on the Erie Canal. John then went to live with his mother, and he attended high school in Victor. He paid his tuition by sweeping the classrooms, building the fires, and ringing the bell.

His teacher organized the more advanced students into a literary society. Every two weeks they met to read articles on various subjects, which they wrote themselves. The older boys wrote speeches, memorized and declaimed them. For a time John was secretary of the society, and later he was elected president.

One day in June, 1848, John's uncle Norton said to him,

"I am going to drive in my carriage to visit your brother in Adam's Basin. Would you like to go with me?" John went along, and it is a good thing that he did. On Sunday of that weekend visit he attended an all-day meeting conducted by Phinehas Smith, an Adventist preacher. John became so interested that, when the minister announced a series of meetings to be held in the town, John decided to attend them. Four years before, at the age of twelve, the boy's heart had been stirred, and he had desired to make a profession of his faith by baptism. The minister had thought him too young, however, and during the following months the desire had been dimmed by worldly activities and studies. God was again calling the youth to give up his worldly ambitions and to follow in the way of the cross.

Before returning with his uncle to Victor, John made plans to attend the meetings. He accepted work in a blacksmith shop, with the understanding that he was to be taught how to build the iron parts of carriages. The prospect of this apprenticeship pleased the youth, for he reasoned that this skill would enable him to help his brother in the carriage-making business. He would earn his expenses working in the shop while he learned a new trade. At the same time he could attend the Adventist meetings, which were to be held every two weeks in a neighborhood schoolhouse.

It was with some feelings of sadness, but with a firm determination to follow the Lord's leading, that he bade his mother and school associates good-by and returned to Adam's Basin.

ANSWERING THE CALL

9

AS SOON as John was acquainted with the work in the blacksmith shop, he was set to work shoeing horses. The shop was operated jointly by two men, Randall and Sparling, and John boarded half the time with one and half the time with the other. Across the street from the shop was a saloon where the men spent much of their leisure time chatting and loafing. This spot did not tempt John, for he kept his Bible close by him in the shop and spent every spare minute in study. The day after he heard a sermon, he would review all the texts and the points emphasized by the minister. Sometimes when the men were in the saloon, and John had no work pressing him, he would go into the coal shed at the back of the shop to pray. While he was praying, the thought would often come to him that he should be baptized. At a prayer meeting in the home of Jonathan Lamson he made his final surrender to God.

One day, Evangelist Smith led two candidates into a deep channel of water above a mill wheel and baptized them into the First-day Adventist Church. John Loughborough was one of the candidates. The sneers and taunts of the men who frequented the blacksmith shop did not disturb him in the least, for his heart overflowed with joy. The only thing that seemed of importance to him was the fact that Jesus was coming soon.

The blacksmith shop stood near the Erie Canal, and back of the shop was a filthy pond of shallow water, made by the overflow from the canal when boats passed. During the summertime this frog pond was a breeding place for malarial mosquitoes. By the middle of September John's system was full of malaria germs. He had not received a single lesson in "ironing wagons" since he began work in the shop. He had not had an opportunity to see one iron rim put on a wagon wheel. In fact, only one carriage had come into the shop all summer. The chief business was horse shoeing.

Day after day John had worked to the point of exhaustion blowing the old-fashioned bellows and striking the anvil with a heavy sledge. His full wages for three months' work making horseshoe nails and shoeing the heavy canal horses was board and lodging and a calfskin apron. He was exhausting his strength, and disease was attacking him; he felt that he could go on no longer. Penniless, malaria-ridden, and thoroughly discouraged, he went home to his mother. She nursed him through the severe chills, bathed his aching head, and prayed with him. At first the chills came every other day, and then every day. Each time when the chill struck, he was impressed that he should tell others the precious truths he had learned from the Bible. When the chill passed and he was up again, he would say to himself, "How can a boy preach who is not yet seventeen years old?" One day he had two chills within twenty-four hours, and the attacks were so severe he thought he was going to die. While praying, he again heard a voice speaking to him. He answered, "Lord, break these chills and fever, and I will go out and preach as soon as I recover sufficient strength to do so." The chills ceased that day.

Now he began to wonder how God would open the way for him to preach. He was without money and necessary clothing, and he was physically exhausted from his nine weeks of malarial fever. He tried to dig a patch of potatoes in order to earn some money, but he had to give it up because of weakness. After resting a few days, he accepted a job sawing and splitting firewood for a neighbor. He boarded with the family, working when his strength would permit. When he was too weak to cut wood, he prepared Bible studies to give as soon as he was ready to start preaching. After a few weeks of convalescing and working, he managed to save one dollar above his expenses!

What should he do for clothing? The neighbor for whom he had been splitting wood gave him a vest and a pair of trousers. But, as he was a man of large proportions, both vest and trousers were about four sizes too large for John. Even after seven inches had been cut off the bottom of the trousers, they were far from a good fit. His brother gave him one of his well-worn dress coats, one of the old-fashioned kind with tails. These were ripped off, and by overlapping the coat in front, it made a double-breasted overcoat that fitted fairly well. With this curious outfit and one dollar in his pocket, he decided to start out. His brother was the only one whom he informed of his decision. He would begin in a place some distance from home, and if he failed, no one in the home town would know of the venture. If God gave him success, he would know that he was following the line of duty.

One day a Mr. Boughton, who had been one of his father's close friends, came to visit him and asked, "John, what are you going to do this winter?"

The youth answered, "There is a man who wants me to work for him in his carriage shop, but he is poor pay. He has not even paid me for work I did for him during the vacation."

"Yes," said Boughton, "but *what* are you going to do?"

"My brother has asked me to board with him and go to school, doing chores for my board."

"Yes," he repeated, "but what *are* you going to do?"

At that, the young man frankly replied, "Brother Boughton, I have decided to go west of Rochester, north of the Ridge Road, and try to preach." John looked down at his well-worn shoes, expecting his friend to say, "Foolishness!"

To his surprise a smile lighted the usually serious face as the good brother replied, "Thank the Lord! that is what I have expected you to do—to become a minister of the gospel."

He told a story that John had never heard before. "One day when you were less than two years old," the man began, "I was visiting at your father's house and you were playing around on the floor. He was telling me what he hoped to make of your older brother and sister. The boy was to become a good mechanic, and the girl a teacher. I asked, 'Nathan, what is the little fellow going to be?' In a solemn manner he replied, 'Brother Boughton, that little fellow is going to help sound the gospel trumpet.' I have been watching you all these years, and I am glad you are going out to preach." Then, after a minute's thought, he asked, "You have been sick. How are you off for money?"

"Well," said John, "I have been able to save one dollar from my wages. This will pay my way to Rochester and leave me twenty-five cents. I'll walk the rest of the way to Kendall Corners, New York, and begin work there."

The kindhearted man reached into his pocket and drew out three dollars, saying as he handed it to John, "This will help you on your way." His encouraging words and the three dollars meant much to the young man. They seemed to assure him that he was doing God's will in starting out to preach the gospel.

A few days after Christmas, shortly before his seventeenth birthday, John boarded a train for Rochester, with a five-dollar package of Adventist tracts under his arm, which his brother had given him to sell and apply on his expenses. From Rochester he walked about ten miles to Adam's Basin, where he spent the night with his brother. Here he must have acquired a small satchel in which he carried tracts, his Bible, hymnbook, and a few personal belongings.

On the last day of the year, after an early breakfast and a season of prayer with his brother, John resumed his journey on foot to Kendall Corners, a distance of fifteen miles. As he neared the village, a wave of loneliness and fear swept over him; but he whispered a prayer. He did not know anyone in the place and had no idea where to go or what to do. Only once in his life before had he spent a night among strangers. As he finished his silent prayer, a man passed him in a cutter. John waved to him, and he stopped.

"Can you tell me if there are any Adventists living in this village?" asked the pedestrian.

"A family of Adventists named Thompson are living in that house across the road," the man replied.

"Thank you, sir," said John.

John made the call, introducing himself as an Adventist preacher. The family eyed him curiously. The youth's heart was pounding hard. What should he answer if they were to ask him what church or organization he represented, or how long he had been preaching? Again he offered a silent prayer, and was happy to hear Mr. Thompson say, "We are glad there can be some Adventist preaching in this village." Then they welcomed him in and asked him to take off his overcoat and cap.

He was greatly embarrassed when his kind hostess urged him to take off his overcoat, for he had to tell her it was the only coat he had. It must have taken some grit and endurance for that young man to walk the ten miles from Rochester to Adam's Basin, and then another fifteen miles from Adam's Basin on to Kendall Corners, in the middle of the winter, with only one coat on, and it well worn! How the cold must have crept up under those loose trousers! Since he had no gloves, we wonder how he kept his hands warm and at the same time carried his satchel. In later years he could not remember any special discomfort, for such inconveniences were thought to be of little consequence in those days.

The Thompsons were friendly and warmhearted. They treated him like a member of their family, yet with the respect due a minister of the gospel. John enjoyed his supper, and he slept soundly on a feather bed that night. Before retiring, he asked Mr. Thompson if he knew of any good place where meetings could be held. The old gentleman replied, "Perhaps the Baptist minister will let you have his meetinghouse; he is quite liberal-minded. I cannot go with you to arrange for the meetings, because of my infirmities; but I'll direct you to his house."

Early on New Year's morning, 1849, John called upon the minister and accepted the invitation to visit in the study. One side of the room was lined with shelves well filled with books. The sight of such an array of volumes almost overawed the young preacher, whose entire library consisted of his Bible, a hymnal, a few tracts, and one or two other books. The minister told him that he would allow him to speak in the church, provided the three trustees gave their consent. John looked up the trustees, who lived some miles apart; and after gaining their consent, he went to the schoolhouse to make his announcement. He knew that the children could carry the news of the meetings to their parents and neighbors as they went home from school that afternoon.

On the evening of January 2, John preached his first sermon, to a well-filled church. He sang a hymn, offered prayer, and then sang again. He told the story of the Garden of Eden, of Adam and Eve's disobedience, and of their great loss because of disobedience. Banished from their perfect home, their life became one of hardship and toil. They were told that they must die and return to the dust. Angels were stationed at the garden gate to prevent them from returning to eat the fruit of the tree of life. No sinner would be permitted access to that fruit; therefore no sinner would live forever. As the guilty pair heard the pronouncement of their punishment, they also received the cheering promise of a Redeemer.

Attentive faces in John's audience assured him that God had used him that night to speak His message as the Holy

Spirit impressed hearts. His natural timidity left him as he broke the bread of life to hungry souls. He did not know until afterward that there were seven preachers in his audience listening to his sermon.

On the second night the church was filled to overflowing. Again the people listened attentively as the young evangelist explained God's plan of salvation and described the home of the saved. He took time to prove every statement from the Scriptures. At the close of the sermon the Baptist minister arose and announced that a series of singing classes was to begin the next evening in the church, and for that reason there would be no more preaching there.

Up jumped Mr. Thompson, son of John's aged host. "Mr. Loughborough," he said, in a voice that arrested the attention of everyone in the room, "this singing class has been planned for the purpose of closing your meetings. I live in a school district five miles south of here. We have a large schoolhouse, and I am one of the trustees. We have consulted together about the matter, and I am authorized to invite you to come and hold meetings there as long as you wish. My home is near the schoolhouse, and you are welcome at our house as long as you desire to stay."

Mr. Loughborough thanked his friend heartily, and said, "Please make an appointment for me to speak in your schoolhouse tomorrow evening." As the two men walked out of the church together, John said in a low voice to his new friend, "They 'can do nothing against the truth, but for the truth.'"

Father Thompson felt greatly embarrassed when he learned of the minister's unfriendly actions. He knew that his attitude was the result of the general opposition of the church people in that vicinity to the Adventist doctrines.

The next morning, as John was getting ready to start for the Thompson schoolhouse, a young boy knocked at the door with a request that John accompany him to his parents' home in the village. A number of persons had gathered there, he said, and they wanted Mr. Loughborough to talk with them. John went with the boy, and when they reached the house they entered by a side door. The front part of the house was a carpenter shop.

They found a number of ladies in the room discussing the meeting of the previous evening. While they were talking, a door from the carpenter shop opened and the man of the house entered, accompanied by the minister. Loughborough tells of his experience with the minister:

"He opened conversation by saying, 'You had a large congregation last evening.' I replied, 'Yes, and they seemed to be interested in what I had to say.' 'Well,' said he, 'I don't know about that; I guess they had a curiosity to hear a boy preach.' I said, 'I think they listened with interest.' He continued by inquiring, 'Did I understand you to say that the soul is not immortal?' I said, 'I do not know how you understood me; I said so.' 'Well,' said he, 'what do you do with the text which says, "These shall go away into everlasting punishment, the death that never dies"?' I replied, 'I do not know of any such text of Scripture. Half of your quotation is in the Bible, and the other half is in the Methodist hymnbook.'

"With much earnestness he said, 'I tell you what I quoted is in the Bible. It is in the twenty-fifth chapter of Revelation.' I said, 'Half of your quotation is in the twenty-fifth chapter of Matthew. It there says of the wicked that they shall go into "everlasting punishment;" but in 2 Thessalonians 1:8, 9 it is called "everlasting destruction." Their fate is destruction, from which they never arise, so it is an "everlasting punishment."' 'Oh, yes,' said he, 'that is all right, but the text I quoted, I tell you, is in the twenty-fifth chapter of Revelation.' I said, 'I presume it is about three chapters outside of the Bible, for there are only twenty-two chapters in Revelation.' He then affirmed again that it was in the twenty-fifth chapter of Revelation, and reached out his hand and said, 'Let me take your Bible, I will show it to you.' I handed him the Bible, and to the astonishment of all he began to turn over the leaves of the Old Testament, and inquired of me, 'Where is Revelation?' I said, 'Look near the last cover of the Bible. It is the last book, and you see there are but twenty-two chapters in the book.' In much confusion he arose and said, 'I would like to stay and talk with you; but I have an engagement.' In much confusion he left the room.

"Those present were greatly astonished. One lady spoke and said, 'I thought he was a learned man; I am astonished.' I said, 'Ladies, he has a large library, and he is a learned man in those books; but he has failed to study his Bible.'"

Though he was an educated man, with many books, he had failed to study his Bible with carefulness. He had taken for granted that the doctrines his church had always taught were correct. Never again was John Loughborough overawed at the sight of a large library in any minister's study. He was satisfied that the simple truths of God's word could cut through all the errors of denominational creeds.

FACING NEW LIGHT

∽10∾

WHEN John Loughborough started out to preach, he had five sermons. During the first few weeks of his labor, by diligent study, he added six more to the list. Thus he was able to give eleven Bible lectures in one place before he moved on to another community. Since he was working alone, he had to make all the arrangements for churches or schoolhouses. He must find a place of meeting, secure permission to use it, and send out the announcements. Sometimes he had to make the fire and arrange the chairs or benches. If he had not already found lodging with some family, he must arrange for that after the meeting was over.

One night he lighted the fire in a schoolhouse where he was to speak and waited for his audience; but no one came. "The next morning, with grip in hand, I started on farther west, not knowing where I should stop or what I should find. About noon I came to a large stone schoolhouse, called the 'Two-bridge Schoolhouse.' I was impressed that there would be a good place for meetings. I called at the nearest house. They gave me my dinner and pointed out where the trustees lived. I saw them, and had an appointment given out in the school. The house was filled the first night. At the close of the discourse I told the people I was a stranger there and would be pleased to receive entertainment with some of them. A Mr. Beardsley, who lived only a little way from the schoolhouse, arose and said, 'Come home with me. You are welcome to make your home there as long as you stay.' He became interested at the first discourse, . . . and accepted all the truths I presented during my stay in the district. It was fine sleighing and moonlight nights, and I had a packed house every evening."

Mr. Loughborough gave his series of eleven lectures in that place, covering briefly the entire plan of salvation from the sin in Eden to the second coming of Christ and the signs of His coming. After this series he returned home for a short rest. He also had the opportunity to supply his mother with firewood for the remainder of the winter. He told his experiences to the Adventist group in Victor, and they encouraged him to continue the work. They gave him money to help meet his expenses and promised to pray for his success. As they handed the young man the few dollars they were able to raise, Brother Boughton said, "Remember the apostle Paul's advice to Timothy, 'Let no man despise thy youth.'"

After a few weeks at home, John started on another preaching tour, visiting Parma and Clarkson. It was only a few miles from Clarkson to Kendall Corners, so John sent out an announcement that he would speak again at the Thompson schoolhouse, promising to answer the question, "Has God given to all men immortality?" The school building was well filled. One of the young men in the congregation was a noisy rowdy. He not only made fun of the speaker, but pelted him with corn and hickory nuts. It was with some difficulty that Loughborough managed to stay on his feet until the sermon was completed. Afterward he learned that a definite plan had been made to break up his meetings.

Fearing that he could accomplish little good working alone under those circumstances, he returned home to counsel with his brethren. They advised him to go with some older minister until he had gained more experience. For three weeks he worked with Phinehas Smith, the man who had baptized him. By that time warm weather had arrived and farmers were busy. Then, too, his brother in Adam's Basin was ill with malaria and requested John to take over his business for the summer.

In November of the same year the Adventist brethren arranged for Loughborough to go on a tour with Evangelist Sullivan Heath, who traveled with horse and carriage. They went together as far as Pennsylvania, stopping along the way wherever they could find a suitable place to hold meetings and distribute tracts. As a result of their winter's labor a number of new believers were added to the Adventist groups.

In the spring of 1850 several church groups joined in raising a fund to purchase a horse, harness, and a light wagon for Loughborough's use. This outfit enabled him to travel from village to village in western New York and to carry a good supply of tracts. He labored in this way for two years, preaching a few sermons in one place and then hastening on to give the message in other communities. In order to earn a few dollars to apply on his expenses he sometimes worked at odd jobs during the day, helping a farmer, mechanic, or carpenter; in the evenings he would preach.

In 1851, at the age of twenty, a little more than three years after he had started preaching, John was married to Mary J. Walker, who loved the Lord with all her heart. She was cheerful under difficulties, always ready to lay aside her plans in order to entertain her husband's friends or accompany him in making his visits to those in need.

John and Mary settled in the city of Rochester, where he became a house painter. Five and a half days each week, for three weeks at a time, he would paint houses. On Saturday afternoon he would drive to one of the three churches under his care, preach the next forenoon, visit the members in the afternoon, and return home that night. Often Mary would go with him on these trips. On the fourth week of the month he would preach in Rochester. He could then work six entire days, because no time was spent in traveling. Late in the summer he became a salesman for Arnold's patent window-sash locks. The commission on his sales brought him sufficient money to enable him to maintain his home and pay his traveling expenses.

The majority of the Adventist people to whom he was preaching still believed that the sanctuary which was cleansed at the end of the twenty-three hundred years was this earth. But John Loughborough could not believe that this was true. He reasoned that if the earth were the sanctuary, then the Lord would have come to cleanse it by fire in 1844, at the time when the prophecy said the sanctuary was to be cleansed. In his daily Bible study he sought an answer to the question, What and where is the sanctuary about which the angel instructed Daniel? He also tried to find some Bible authority for keeping Sunday holy, but failed to find it. The Adventists were preaching the first and second angels' messages; but what about the third? Why was that neglected? What was the two-horned beast of Revelation 13? Had God's law been abolished, as the Adventists taught? If so, why was it necessary to keep any day holy?

Only once had Loughborough attempted to speak publicly on the subject of God's law. In the course of his sermon he read Christ's statement found in Matthew 5:18: "Till heaven and earth pass, one jot or one tittle shall in nowise pass from the law, till all be fulfilled." As he read the passage to his congregation, the words came into his mind as distinctly as if spoken by an audible voice: "Heaven and earth have not passed away yet." He was so confused that he did not know how to proceed. To gain time, he read the text again, with added emphasis; but again he seemed to hear the voice: "Heaven and earth have not passed away yet." He passed lightly over the remaining points in his sermon, and finished with difficulty.

When he sat down he said to himself, "I will never speak on that subject again until the law question is clearer in my mind than it is now." He could not harmonize the words of Christ, "Think not that I am come to destroy the law, or the prophets," with Paul's statement that the handwriting of ordinances was nailed to the cross.

He told the leading brethren in the Adventist groups at Clarkson and Parma, with whom he held Sunday meetings, about some of the difficulties he had met and some of the questions that had arisen in his mind. He asked them to pray that God would send light. The Lord answered their prayer and sent light, but not in exactly the way that Loughborough expected.

One day in September, 1852, after John Loughborough had returned to Rochester from a short preaching tour, Mr. Orton, one of his friends, came to him. Speaking of a meeting to be held that night, he said, "Your Clarkson and Parma companies have all joined the seventh-day people, and you have a duty to go to that meeting and get them out of the Saturdaykeeping." He explained that the minister would give the congregation an opportunity to ask questions, and he added, "You get your texts ready to show them that the law is abolished."

That night these two men, with six others of the group, attended the meeting of the seventh-day people. It was held in the front room of a large rented house on Mount Hope Avenue, which served as mission home, publishing house, and church. John Loughborough was prepared for a stiff argument, and his proof texts were copied on a slip of paper in his Bible.

When the group reached the building, they found that a conference was in session. They entered the room while a testimony meeting was in progress. Testimonies of praise came from loving hearts, and the visitors were impressed by the heavenly atmosphere of the meeting. In a few minutes Harvey Cottrell entered and stood up to give his testimony. "Praise the Lord for His goodness," he said as his face beamed. "I came to Rochester last Tuesday to attend this Bible conference, but have been in bed with a fever. My great desire to be with you led me to ask the brethren to anoint me and pray for my healing, according to the instructions in the fifth chapter of James; and *I am here!*"

Loughborough remembered that his own uncle, an earnest Christian and a devout Adventist, had been healed in

Facing New Light

the same way only a few weeks before. He said to himself, "The stories that were told me about the seventh-day people getting together and having a noisy, fanatical time, screaming and yelling, must be false. Their meetings are quiet and dignified; and it can be seen that the blessing of the Lord is with them."

When the time came for the preaching service, John Andrews, a young man not much older than John Loughborough, arose and said, "I had prepared to speak on a certain subject, but during this social meeting my mind had turned to another subject. It may be the will of the Lord that I take that subject. It is to speak of the texts supposed to teach that the Ten Commandments were abolished at the cross." He began by reading Colossians 2:14-17, the first text that Mr. Loughborough had set down on his list!

"Blotting out the handwriting of ordinances, . . . nailing it to His cross." He read the four verses and then added, "There are two laws, the great moral law of Ten Commandments, which is to exist through endless ages, and the law that consisted of ceremonies that pointed forward to Christ, and which ceased at the cross. The law of Ten Commandments was graven on tablets of stone by the finger of God. The handwriting of ordinances was made by Moses on parchments. *Blotting out* would not be a correct figure relative to that law engraven on stone, but might be appropriate when applied to temporal regulations, written on parchment with ink and pen.

"One of these regulations that were said to be 'against us' and 'contrary to us' commanded, 'Three times in a year shall all thy males appear before' Me, in Jerusalem. Such a law could be easily carried out in the land of Palestine, but would not be applicable in the gospel work, with its believers scattered to earth's remotest bounds; so that law is taken 'out of the way.' The law that was blotted out was the ceremonial law. It consisted of rules and regulations pertaining to the sacrifices and services of the tabernacle, which pointed forward to the Lamb of God, the divine sacrifice. When Christ offered up His life on the cross, these ceremonial sacrifices ceased and the laws pertaining to them were in figure nailed to the cross."

"So there are two laws," said John Loughborough to himself. "I had never thought of that. It does make things clearer. But if this text does not refer to the Ten Commandment law, why does it say in verse 16 that we are not to let anyone judge us in respect of the *sabbath days?*"

The speaker, seemingly guided by the Holy Spirit, took up that point next. He read Leviticus 23, about the seven yearly sabbaths which the Lord commanded the children of Israel to observe. "These sabbaths are plainly shown to be distinct from the Sabbath of the fourth commandment," he said, "and have ceased because the law commanding their observance is blotted out."

"That all seems reasonable," said John Loughborough to himself, as he struck Colossians 2:14-17 off his list. He looked at his next text, Ephesians 2:13-15, and the question came into his mind, "Does not this say that Christ 'abolished' the 'law of commandments'? I wonder what our friend will say about that text?" He listened. Could it be possible? The speaker was reading that very scripture. As he read it, Andrews asked, "What law is spoken of here? We are told plainly that it is 'the law of commandments contained in ordinances,' that is, the rules and regulations pertaining to

Facing New Light 63

the sacrifices, not the moral law of Ten Commandments by which all God's children must test their lives."

By this time, John Loughborough and his friends who had come with him began to see that their no-law theory was sliding sand. Orton had been convinced of this fact for some time, but had tactfully concealed his new opinions until he could persuade his friend to attend the meeting and hear the seventh-day people present their views.

To Loughborough it seemed clearly to be a matter of divine guidance that the speaker should continue reading text after text that was listed in the listener's notes. The speaker carefully examined every one of the texts and showed that not one of them proved the law of Ten Commandments to be abolished. At last he called attention to Matthew 5:17-19, the scripture which had caused the young preacher confusion and embarrassment the night he had tried to speak on the subject of the law. Said Mr. Andrews, "Every letter and point of a letter is to stand until Christ comes, . . . and until all God's prophecies have been fulfilled."

In speaking of the evening's experience, Loughborough later reminisced, "It was to me like a grand door opening into a region of light." He rejoiced and thanked God for it, yet he felt there was much more to learn. Andrews had spoken of the heavenly sanctuary. Was the sanctuary *in heaven?* Most Christian people took it for granted that the sanctuary was this earth, or was somewhere on this earth. Perhaps these people understood some things about the sanctuary and its cleansing that would throw light on the disappointment of 1844.

As soon as the meeting closed, father Lamson, in whose

home John had made his final surrender to Christ before his baptism, and who had done much to encourage him to be a minister, came and greeted Loughborough. He threw his arms around the young man and asked, "Brother John, does not that subject look pretty clear?"

"Yes, it does."

"You will have to keep the Sabbath, won't you?"

John's prompt answer was, "Brother Lamson, unless I can find something stronger than what I had supposed teaches the abolition of the law of the Ten Commandments, I shall have to keep the Sabbath."

This was the last night of the conference; but, since a number of persons wanted the Bible studies to continue, young Andrews appointed meetings each night for a week. Loughborough and his friends attended these classes, and they also studied together in their homes during the day. They gladly accepted the truths that their teacher presented from the Bible, and they carried them to their associates. Some refused to make the sacrifice of adopting an unpopular change of worship from Sunday to Saturday. There were some who made every attempt to keep their brethren from joining the Sabbathkeepers, and, failing in this, they frequently resorted to ridicule and abuse.

AN EVIL SPIRIT REBUKED

11

THE door into the region of light opened wider and wider for John Loughborough as he studied with the Bible class taught by John Andrews. Before a week had passed, he understood the "two-horned beast," the "third angel's message," and "the mark of the beast." The young man had made up his mind to keep the Sabbath of the fourth commandment; but he did not tell any of his friends of his decision until he was sure he could give a good answer to all objections. He had appointments already made for three weeks in outlying churches, but on the fourth Sabbath after hearing the message he took his stand publicly with the Mount Hope Avenue group for the Bible Sabbath.

It was here at this time that Loughborough first met Elder James White and his wife Ellen. They had been traveling with their horse and carriage for about three months, going as far as Bangor, Maine. They had held meetings and visited scattered Sabbathkeepers along the way.

Oswald Stowell, the young man who ran the hand press on which the church paper, the *Review and Herald*, was printed, had become seriously ill with pleurisy. His physician had given him up to die. During the Sabbath meeting he was in an adjoining room, suffering agonizing pain. At the close of the meeting he requested that prayer be offered for him. Elder and Mrs. White asked John Loughborough to go with them into the sickroom. The three bowed in prayer, while the rest of the company prayed silently in the meeting room. Elder White anointed Stowell, and when they arose from their knees, the patient was sitting up in bed. Striking his sides that had been so painful a few minutes before, he declared, "I am fully healed. I shall be able to work the hand press tomorrow." He did run it two days later.

At this moment they noticed that Mrs. White had not risen from her knees. Her husband looked at her and said, "Ellen is in vision." Her eyes were open, and she seemed to be gazing at something in the distance. Her face did not look pale, but appeared as fresh and natural as usual. She was looking upward, moving her head from side to side as if viewing various objects. She seemed to notice nothing that was going on around her. Her hands moved gracefully from time to time, pointing in the direction in which she was looking. Then, perhaps the next moment, they would be clasped upon her breast.

Elder White said, "She does not breathe while in this condition. If any of you desire to satisfy yourselves of this fact, you are at liberty to examine her." Some of the people at the meeting came into the room. They found that her pulse was beating regularly, yet, by the closest examination, they could not detect any breath in her body. Occasionally she spoke, sometimes single words, sometimes sentences, as if she were talking with someone. After about half an hour she drew three deep breaths, like those of a newborn babe

An Evil Spirit Rebuked

filling its lungs for the first time. Soon she began to tell those around her what she had seen in vision.

Turning to John Loughborough, she said, "I saw three men trying hard to keep you from joining the Sabbath-keeping Adventists. I heard unkind words spoken to you by your fellow ministers." She even told him what his thoughts had been while he was reaching the decision to keep the Sabbath—thoughts which he had not expressed to anyone, not even to his wife. As he heard these words from her lips he said to himself, "Surely there is a power more than human connected with this vision."

In the company that day was a Mrs. Riggs, who seemed to be in great mental suffering. The sisters in the group had often asked her to tell them her difficulty so that they might help her, but she had never answered a word. When Mrs. White was relating the vision, she said to this sister, "I saw you in deep trouble, and that you will not tell anyone what the trouble is. . . . I was told to say to you, 'If you will confess your trouble and have the brethren and sisters pray for you, the Lord will hear prayer and rebuke the power of Satan, and you will have no more of this trouble."

Although Mrs. White urged the sister to tell what her trouble was, and asked the whole company to pray for her, not a word came from the woman's lips. She continued to stare with the same anxious expression on her face. After waiting for her to speak, Mrs. White said to her, "I was also shown that after you retire for the night, and extinguish the light, there appears to you what looks like an old woman dressed in black, and it terrifies you. This apparition threatens that if you tell anybody, she will choke you to death. When you are in the presence of your sisters you think you will tell them all about it and have them pray for you that the Lord may rebuke this work of Satan. But you fear to tell them of your trial lest the spirit carry out its threat and take your life. Sister Riggs, I have been shown that if you take your stand against this power and have the brethren and sisters pray for you, it will be rebuked, and you will never be troubled with it again."

That afternoon Mrs. White called at the home of Mr. Orton and found Mrs. Loughborough, Mrs. Riggs, and several other members present. Sister White said, "Now, Sister Riggs, this is a good time for you to take your position against that spirit which is troubling you, and we will unite in prayer for you." Sister Riggs spoke two words, "It is—" At once she began to struggle as though she was trying to tear herself away from the grasp of a strong person. She turned black in the face, but finally succeeded in crying out, "Pray!" Immediately those present engaged in a season of prayer for her. The evil spirit was rebuked and victory came.

After prayer, Mrs. Riggs said, "When Sister White began to talk with me, I thought I would own up to the truthfulness of what she had told me of my case; but the moment I formed the resolution, the apparition was in the corner of the room, shaking her head at me, and saying, 'If you do tell, I will choke you to death.' I thought I would say, 'It is so,' so quickly that she could not choke me; but the moment I spoke a word, as it seemed to me, she had me by the throat, and I was struggling for life. All Sister White said about the case is true. Thank the Lord, He has given me the victory."

Before this trying experience had come to Mrs. Riggs, she had, several times, sat in a circle with spirit mediums, and she had listened to supposed communications from the dead.

An Evil Spirit Rebuked

By attending these spirit séances she had placed herself in danger. Of her own free will she had sat with those who thought they were talking with their dead friends, but who were actually talking with the evil spirits. Now she was free from their power. Never again did she have anything to do with spiritism.

John Loughborough was well acquainted with the Bible teachings regarding spiritism, for he had many times read the scriptures which state that the dead cannot speak with man. This experience of Mrs. Riggs's impressed him deeply. He better understood God's loving care over His people in warning them again and again to have nothing to do with those who try to talk with the dead.

He was interested to learn that, two years before this, Mrs. White had been given a vision in which she was shown that Satan would try to deceive the whole world through the influence of these evil spirits. Here are a few words from this vision, as she wrote it in 1850:

"Satan will have power to bring before us the appearance of forms purporting to be our relatives or friends now sleeping in Jesus. It will be made to appear as if these friends were present; the words that they uttered while here, with which we were familiar, will be spoken, and the same tone of voice that they had while living will fall upon the ear. All this is to deceive the saints and ensnare them into the belief of this delusion."—*Early Writings,* page 87.

After reading this entire vision, John Loughborough better understood the purpose of the evil one in trying to make the world believe that the dead are alive.

From the day that John Loughborough first saw Mrs. White in vision, he was interested in learning more about her and the messages God sent through her. In answer to his many questions, he was given her book, *Christian Experience and Views*. Imagine his delight when, on reading an account of her first vision, he found the answer to the question that had been troubling him: Was 'the midnight cry' from heaven, or was it merely the invention of fanatical men, as some believed? This is a portion of what he read in the book:

"I raised my eyes, and saw a straight and narrow path, cast up high above the world. On this path the advent people were traveling to the city, which was at the farther end of the path. They had a bright light set up behind them at the beginning of the path, which an angel told me was the midnight cry. This light shone all along the path and gave light for their feet so that they might not stumble."—*Early Writings*, page 14.

As Loughborough read the account of this first vision and learned that it was given only two months after the day of expectation passed, he said to himself, "This is a message from Jesus, our great High Priest. It is sent from heaven to cheer His disappointed people." Why, then, he wondered, are so many in darkness? He knew that most of the Adventist people were bewildered and confused. While some, like the Loughborough family, waited patiently, hoping that Jesus would come soon, there were many others who set dates for His return. A large group denied that God had anything to do with the time message of 1844, and some even taught that the coming was spiritual and invisible and that it had already taken place.

John could not understand this confusion. Why could Bible students not see that Jesus had sent them this word,

An Evil Spirit Rebuked

telling them that "the midnight cry" was a bright light and that it would shine all along the path to the Holy City? He was made sad to learn that at a conference held in Albany in 1845 the Adventist leaders had decided that, because there were so many false prophets in the world, they would not listen to anyone claiming to have visions from heaven. He wondered if they had never noticed the Scripture command: "Despise not prophesyings. Prove all things; hold fast that which is good." He made up his mind to test these visions of Mrs. White by the Bible rule, "To the law and to the testimony: if they speak not according to this word, it is because there is no light in them." He now continued reading in the little book, about the experience of the Adventists traveling along the pathway to heaven:

"If they kept their eyes fixed on Jesus, who was just before them, leading them to the city, they were safe. But soon some grew weary, and said the city was a great way off, and they expected to have entered it before. Then Jesus would encourage them by raising His glorious right arm, and from His arm came a light which waved over the advent band, and they shouted, 'Alleluia!' Others rashly denied the light behind them and said that it was not God that had led them out so far. The light behind them went out, leaving their feet in perfect darkness, and they stumbled and lost sight of the mark and of Jesus, and fell off the path down into the dark and wicked world below."—*Early Writings*, pages 14, 15.

That is what many of the Adventists have done, thought John sadly. They have rashly denied that the judgment-hour message given in 1844 was from God. When the time passed, many felt relieved to think that Jesus might not come for a long time. Now they could go on enjoying the pleasures of the world as before.

Along with the book *Christian Experience and Views*, Loughborough read the back numbers of the two papers edited by James White, *The Present Truth* and the *Advent Review*. As he read the articles written by earnest Bible students, other questions which had been troubling him were answered, and the truth stood out clearly.

He saw that the experiences of the Adventists, including their disappointment, had been pictured by the prophet John in the tenth chapter of the Revelation. He read the words of the angel to the ones who were so bitterly disappointed, "Thou must prophesy again before many peoples, and nations, and tongues, and kings," which indicated that their work on earth was not yet finished. They were also told to "Rise, and measure the temple of God," which, we have learned, is His sanctuary. In response to this command they began studying the subject of the sanctuary.

John was especially interested in an article by O. R. L. Crosier, printed in the *Day Star*, January, 1846. In it the writer explained the work of Jesus, our great High Priest in the heavenly sanctuary. John also read Mrs. White's advice to all the believers to read that article because Crosier had found the truth about the sanctuary. He contended that this earth is not the sanctuary and that nowhere in the Bible is the earth called the sanctuary. He showed that the sanctuary which was cleansed at the end of the 2300 years is "the New Jerusalem temple, of which Christ is the minister."

As John continued to study, he learned that the Day of Atonement in the tabernacle service represented the judgment day, and was so called by the people of Israel. While

An Evil Spirit Rebuked

the high priest performed the solemn services of the Day of Atonement inside the tabernacle, the congregation outside were praying and searching their hearts to see if there were any unconfessed sins. All the sins that had been confessed, either during the year or on this special day, were carried away into the land of separation. But the sinner who failed to make confession continued to bear his own sins. He was separated from God's people and had no further part with them.

John had another question to be answered: Was not heaven a pure and holy place? Why should anything there need cleansing? He knew that when we confess our sins God forgives them, but he learned that the record is not at once blotted out of the books of heaven. It is the record of these sins that defiles the heavenly sanctuary. The sanctuary is cleansed by the blotting out of these sins; then the judgment work is finished. Those who have unconfessed sins written against their name will receive the punishment of death; but those whose record is clear will receive the reward of eternal life.

As the young minister continued his reading and studying, he saw clearly that it was the work of cleansing the *heavenly* sanctuary that was begun on the great Day of Atonement, October 22, 1844. Reverently he whispered, "It most certainly is true that Jesus is coming soon, for He has begun the final judgment work. This is the last work He will do in the heavenly sanctuary before He comes to take us home. It was 'the midnight cry' that showed us the day that Jesus began this work. Thank God for this 'bright light' that shines along our path to the city, lighting our way so that we need not stumble."

THE SILVER THREE-CENT PIECE

～12～

WHEN John Loughborough first began selling window-sash locks, he did so well that he soon saved $35. After he began to keep the Sabbath, his sales fell off. He prayed that the Lord would prosper his business; but, while he was praying, the impression came to him that it was his duty to give *all* his time to teaching the Bible truth. God was calling him to the work of preaching the gospel message; but in his heart he would answer, "No, I will work hard and earn money, so that I can support another minister who will be able to do this work better than I can."

He worked long hours, though the harder he worked the fewer sales he made. The builders whom he solicited would say, "We intend to use the Arnold window-sash locks, but we are not ready yet to place the order." Finally his savings were exhausted, and he was earning scarcely enough to pay his hotel bills and traveling expenses to and from the places where his business called him. He came home one weekend with only a silver three-cent piece in his pocket.

It was with a heavy heart that he went to meeting Sabbath morning. It also seemed as if a cloud were resting on the little company who met that day in the Mount Hope Avenue chapel. Prayer was offered that God would lift the cloud and give His blessing.

When he returned home after the morning service, John went alone to his room for prayer. He said, "Lord, if Thou wilt open the way, I will go." Then, as he continued praying, his faith grew stronger, and he said, "I will obey, Lord, and Thou wilt open the way." As soon as he had made this decision, his anxiety left him, and his heart was filled with joy and thanksgiving. He said to himself, "The Lord has told me to go, and the Lord will provide."

Mrs. White was given a vision and a special message for John Loughborough. "He is resisting the conviction of duty," she said. "God wants him to give himself wholly to the preaching of the message."

On the following Monday morning his wife said, "John, can you let me have some money? I must go to town and buy some matches and thread." He reached into his pocket and, bringing out the tiny silver coin, he handed it to her, saying, "Mary, there is a three-cent piece. It is all the money I have in the world. Get only one cent's worth of matches. Do not spend but one of the other two cents. Bring me one cent, so that we shall not be entirely out of money. You know, Mary, I have tried every way in my power to make this business succeed, but I cannot."

Bursting into tears, she said, "John, what in the world are we going to do?"

"I have been powerfully convicted for weeks that the reason my business does not succeed is because the Lord's hand is against me for neglecting duty," he replied. "It is my duty to give myself wholly to preaching the truth."

"But, if you go to preaching, how are we to be supported?"

Then he reminded her of the Sabbath vision, and of God's call to him. "Well, as soon as I decided to obey the call of duty," he explained, "there came to me the assurance that the Lord is going to open the way. I don't know *how* it will be done, but the way will open."

Mary went to her room to have a good cry and to do some praying. Then she put on her coat and went to town.

About half an hour after she had gone, there was a knock at the door. John left his Bible open on the table where he had been studying, went to the door, and invited the stranger to come in. After the two had exchanged greetings, the stranger said, "I am Mr. ——, from Middleport. I am not in very good health, and am going to the State of Ohio for my health. I wish to take along some small business with which to meet expenses. I have been recommended to you by Mr. Thomas Garbut, to purchase some of Mr. Arnold's patent sash locks. I want $80 worth of locks and will leave you to pick out an assortment. . . . I will take the locks tomorrow and pay you the money."

Loughborough's wholesale commission on those locks was one third the gross receipts, or more than $26. This amount of cash would be his earnings for the slight trouble of walking half a mile to the factory and leaving the order. In those days $26 would buy nearly ten times what it will today.

When Mary returned with the matches and thread and the one cent, she found her husband singing. "You seem to be very happy," she observed.

"While you were gone, the way was opened for me to go

out and preach." Then he told her what had happened while she was absent.

Tears again filled Mary's eyes, and she went to her room, this time to thank the Lord for sending help. Soon she came back, ready to do whatever she could to help John prepare to preach. With the $26 he bought firewood and provisions, and other needed comforts for the home.

On the next Sabbath there was a gathering of the Sabbathkeepers from western New York. John Loughborough tells the story of what happened that day:

"Brother Hiram Edson, who lived some forty miles east of Rochester, had decided not to attend that meeting; but his wife had been so impressed that he was going to be called away that she had all his clothing in shape for any emergency. On the said Sabbath morning, while engaged in family worship, the impression came upon him as strong as though spoken with an audible voice, 'Go to Rochester, you are wanted there.' He said to his wife, 'What does that mean? I do not know why I should go to Rochester.' All the day the impression came stronger and stronger. Several times in the day he retired to his barn to pray, and every time the impression would come, 'Go to Rochester.'

"Finally he said to Sister Edson, 'Is my clothing in a condition to leave? It is my impression that I am to be gone several weeks.' She assured him that all was ready, for she had been impressed that he would be called somewhere. After the close of the Sabbath he took the cars for Rochester. On arriving at Mount Hope Avenue about nine o'clock at night, he said to Brother White, 'I did not expect to come to this meeting, but I have been impressed so strongly today that I should come here that here I am. What do you want of me?' 'Well,' said Brother White, 'we want you to take old Charlie horse and the carriage and take Brother Loughborough around on your six-weeks' circuit in southwestern New York and Pennsylvania, and get him started in preaching the third angel's message.' "

On December 20, 1852, Charlie was harnessed to the carriage, and the two men, Hiram Edson and John Loughborough, started on their tour, visiting scattered companies and families of Sabbathkeepers. On their first Sabbath out, at Orangeport, there was a heavy snow, which made it impossible for them to use the carriage. "We'll fix you up for traveling over the snow," said their host. Early Sunday morning he set to work, and with the help of other members of the family he soon manufactured a "pung," a strong wooden box with runners fastened to the bottom of it. To this queer conveyance Charlie was harnessed, and the two men climbed into it with their satchels and packages of books and tracts. They went on their way, leaving the carriage until their return.

On Christmas Day the pung drove into Buffalo in a driving snowstorm. It must have been a cold ride, especially for Mr. Loughborough, who had no overcoat until generous Hiram Edson stopped at a store and bought one for him.

Friday afternoon the Hacket family, who were waiting for the arrival of the ministers, were surprised to see a horse trot briskly into the yard drawing an improvised sled. Soon the two men were handing their satchels to their host, who greeted them warmly. "Welcome, brethren," he said as he helped them into the house. "We are happy to have you with us, and to know that our fellow townsmen are to have the opportunity of hearing the reasons of our faith from a

The Silver Three-Cent Piece 79

real preacher. You know we are the only Adventist family living here in State Line settlement. The big schoolhouse is engaged for Sunday afternoon and evening. I also tried to get the morning hour for you, but arrangements had already been made for another minister to speak then."

On Sunday morning John Loughborough and Hiram Edson accompanied Lewis Hacket and his family to the schoolhouse to listen to the "other minister;" but he did not appear. Loughborough was asked to occupy the pulpit. As he stepped forward he was somewhat embarrassed by the curious manner in which the members of the congregation stared at him. They paid good attention, however, and most of them returned in the afternoon and again in the evening, bringing so many of their friends with them that the house was packed.

As Loughborough stepped into the Hacket shoeshop on Monday morning, he caught sight of a handbill announcing the Sunday meetings. This is what he read: "J. N. Loughborough, of Rochester, will speak in the schoolhouse on Sunday at 2 and 7 p.m. Come and hear, for 'these that have turned the world upside down are come hither also,' whom Lewis hath received. And these do all contrary to the decrees of the pope, saying that there is a better way—the commandments of God and the faith of Jesus."

"Is that the way you notified this town?" asked John Loughborough. "If so, I can readily understand the curious look of the audience when I first came before them."

"Well," said Lewis Hacket, "I was bound to get the townspeople to hear, and I thought that would draw them."

After several weeks of traveling and preaching, Loughborough and Edson were ready to start home. The snow was fast melting and, by the time they were within forty miles of Rochester, it had disappeared. The men had to walk most of the forty miles to make it easier for Charlie to draw the pung over the dry ground. From Rochester, Mr. Edson went by train back to his farm; and John mounted Charlie with the harness on, and rode fifty miles to Orangeport to get the carriage. They had been on the trip about six weeks, and during that time had visited a dozen or more companies of Sabbathkeepers as well as many scattered families. Thus ended John Loughborough's first preaching tour for what was later known as the Seventh-day Adventist denomination.

The ministers met some strange people in those days. A man came into the meetings at Rochester, who claimed to have reached a position where he could never be tempted to sin. One Sabbath he was the first to speak in a testimony meeting. He said, "Brethren, come up on the platform that I am on. *Come up! Come up!*" While John Loughborough was waiting to see what would happen next, Elder James White arose to his feet, and said, "Brother, you speak of being up on some platform. It reminds me of a man of small stature in Christ's time who wanted to see the Saviour, so he ran ahead, and climbed up into a sycamore tree. When the Saviour came along, He said, 'Zacchaeus, make haste, and come down.' . . . I will now say to you, Zacchaeus, come down. . . . I tell you that you have sat down on the easy stool of the devil, where you will think that all your impressions are from the Lord, and you will be led into gross sins."

A few weeks later this man brought a young woman home with him. He announced to his wife, who was busy getting supper, that she must leave the house and take her two-month-old baby with her, because he had a new wife. It wasn't long until the city authorities took the man to jail.

On one of his tours, Loughborough lodged overnight with a family where the husband felt impressed that the Lord wanted him to preach. He was a good singer, and he liked music. That evening, while his wife was splitting firewood with which to cook the supper, he sat in an easy chair with his feet on another chair, singing with gusto, "We'll have nothing at all to do but to march around Jerusalem, when we arrive at home." Loughborough went out into the yard and took the ax from the wife's hands, while her husband continued his singing, scarcely aware of what was going on.

Doubtless John gave this man no encouragement in his ambition to go out preaching; and probably he warned him of the danger of blindly following every impression that might come to him. Loughborough often said, "The true Christian will reject every impression that is not in harmony with the teachings of God's word and the Spirit of Christ. The Holy Spirit is not imparted to those who are too careless to seek to become acquainted with the instruction God has given, or too willful to obey it. Impressions often come from the evil one. Those who follow impressions blindly are in danger of being deceived by Satan and led astray from the path of duty."

PERPLEXING PROBLEMS

～13～

JOHN LOUGHBOROUGH made his first trip to Michigan in May, 1853. He attended a conference in Jackson, Michigan, in June, where he joined a group of workers who were traveling with Elder and Mrs. White. Elder White was impressed with John's preaching, for this appeared in an editorial in the *Review and Herald:* "Brother J. N. Loughborough preached twice, with clearness, much to the edification of the brethren."

In the home where they were lodging, Loughborough saw Mrs. White intently writing. She explained that she was writing out a vision which the Lord had given her at Tyrone, concerning Sabbathkeepers in Michigan, and especially regarding a certain woman who pretended to be so holy that she did not need the Ten Commandments as a guide. The Lord had shown His servant that this woman was corrupt.

Mr. Loughborough said, "Sister White, I would like a copy of that vision."

"This is written with a pencil," said Mrs. White, "but if you will make a copy with ink for me, you may have the pencil copy." He took the pencil copy, read it, and put it into his pocket.

Perplexing Problems

During the next three weeks the company traveled two hundred miles, visiting churches throughout the state. In the town of Vergennes their host and hostess came out to greet them. Mrs. White whispered to her husband, "James, we have gotten to the place where that woman lives."

He replied, "This is not the family, is it?"

"No," Mrs. White replied, "but I saw these in connection with the case."

Sabbath morning they traveled two miles through timberland to a farm with a house and a new barn. Since the barn was to be the place of meeting, planks had been brought in for seats and a rostrum had been built at the end opposite the door. Elder White preached the sermon, and John Loughborough sat next to Mrs. White on the rostrum.

After the meeting had begun, an old man, a young man, and a tall woman came in. The two men came forward and sat down right in front of the speaker, but the woman took a seat at the back by the door. Holding her fan before her face, Mrs. White whispered to John Loughborough, "Do you see that woman who just sat down by the door? She is the woman that I saw in vision. The old man here is her husband, and the young man in the green coat, sitting beside him, is the one with whom she is traveling around the country. When James gets through speaking, I shall relate the vision, and you will see whether they are the ones described in that copy of it which you have in your pocket."

Elder White spoke only a short time. Then he said, "I think someone else has something to say." Mrs. White arose and read Isaiah 52:11: "Be ye clean, that bear the vessels of the Lord." She spoke of the sacredness of the work of teaching Bible truth, and how careful those who are laboring in public should be in their life and deportment. Then she added, "If the Lord called a woman to the ministry, she would not be traveling around the country with another than her husband." At these words, there was a stir and some whispering in the audience.

Mrs. White continued: "Friends, what I am talking about is right here before us. That tall woman, who came in and sat down by the door a few minutes ago, claims to be very holy. She also claims to have the gift of tongues. The words she rattles off are mere gibberish. She does not talk any language. If every nation on earth heard her, none of them would understand a thing, for she does not talk any language. This woman claims to have a holiness so high that she does not need the Ten Commandments. This old man on the front seat is her husband. God pity him. He toils at home to earn money for her to travel around the country with this young man who sits by his side—supporting them in their iniquity." After a few more words, Mrs. White sat down.

All eyes were turned toward the woman, wondering what she would say. The copy of the vision that was written out three weeks before, and which John Loughborough had been carrying in his pocket, gave the words which the woman would say when she was reproved. It said, "She will put on a very sanctimonious look, and say, 'The Lord knows my heart.'"

After a moment of complete silence the woman rose to her feet and in a solemn manner uttered these five words: "The Lord knows my heart." The meeting was dismissed for the noon-hour recess, while those who had driven their teams in from a distance ate lunch, and the Whites and the group of workers accompanying them went to the farmhouse for dinner.

After lunch the holiness woman gathered those who were in the barn and gave them a talk on holiness. While speaking, she broke off in what she called "tongues." John Loughborough reached the barn in time to hear her mumbling, "Kenne, kenni, kenne kenno, kenne kenne kenne kennioe." She continued for some time repeating these words as fast as her tongue could rattle them off. As the people began to return for the afternoon service, her meeting broke up.

After the workers had gone on their way Sunday, the woman called a meeting in a schoolhouse in the neighborhood. After talking on the subject of holiness she told her audience that the Lord had given her the gift of tongues and that this gift was to fit her to be a missionary to a certain tribe of Indians living a few miles away on the Flat River.

While she was speaking, one of these Indians, who was on a hunting trip, came to the door of the schoolhouse. Some boys sitting near the door saw him and went out and invited him to come in and hear a woman who could talk his language. The Indian hunter took a seat near the door and leaned his gun against the wall. When she saw him, she broke out in her "kenne, kenni." The Indian stared at her, jumped up, grabbed his gun, and rushed out of the house with a whoop! "Very bad Injun that! Very bad Injun that!" The boys followed him and asked, "What did she say?"

"Nothing. She talk no Injun."

This woman was the second wife of the old man and much younger than he. Soon after this, his son, who had no faith in his stepmother's mission to the Indians, took her to an Indian interpreter and had her speak her gibberish for him. When he asked the interpreter what she had said, he answered, "I have been interpreter for seventeen different tribes of Indians, and she has not uttered a single Indian word."

That put an end to the influence of this "holiness preacher." Years afterward the young man accused of sin admitted that all Mrs. White had said about her was true.

God does not bestow His gifts for the idle amusement of the crowds. Elder Loughborough often said, "The Lord gave the gift of tongues to His apostles on the Day of Pentecost to make it possible for them to give the gospel of salvation in one day to thousands of people gathered at Jerusalem from the various language areas of Europe and Asia."

In modern times this gift has, on special occasions, been given to faithful missionaries to enable them to preach or interpret the story of the gospel in languages that they do not know.

ACROSS THE PRAIRIES

~14~

THE conference held in Jackson, Michigan, June 3 to 5, laid plans for advance among the believers. In the *Review and Herald* of June 23, 1853, Elder James White wrote:

"At this meeting a mission to Wisconsin and Illinois was considered. Brethren J. N. Loughborough and M. E. Cornell decided to go in company, with private conveyance. Necessary means to help them in their field of labor were raised at once. We also furnished them with a full supply of tracts, which they will sell to those who can pay, and give to the worthy poor. . . . It is of little use for brethren to fly from place to place, and spend but a few hours or days at each. These brethren design spending months in the West."

The two pioneering ministers separated from the main company of workers and traveled by horse and carriage to Grand Rapids, Michigan, where they held evangelistic services the following Sabbath and Sunday. Early Monday morning they started for Grand Haven, on the shore of Lake Michigan, for they planned to take the steamer across the lake to Illinois. Thinking that they would be able to make the drive in a few hours, they took only a small lunch with them. It was some forty miles, however, and the travelers became very hungry. Imagine their delight when on their journey they found the ground covered with wintergreen plants. They gathered berries by handfuls and satisfied their hunger.

That night they lodged at a hotel in Grand Haven, and the next afternoon drove the horse and carriage onto a steamer. What a time they had with the horse! He was in terror from the noise of the engines and the shrieking of the whistle. He neither ate nor slept during the twenty hours that they were on the steamer.

Finally they reached the west shore of Lake Michigan, at the prairie town of Chicago. There were no paved streets, and the mud was a foot deep. With some difficulty the horse managed to pull the carriage the half mile to higher ground, where the men unharnessed him and let him feed on prairie grass. After that he was ready for his nose bag of oats.

While the horse was eating, the two men sat down on the grass to plan their tour. They had a list of Sabbathkeepers and *Review* subscribers in Illinois and Wisconsin whom they desired to visit. For two days they traveled the country roads over open prairie from Chicago to Alden, Illinois, before they came to the first two families on their list.

It was Friday afternoon when they reached the home of the Chapmans, one of the two families with whom they planned to spend the weekend. Before the travelers arrived they found a patch of ripe wild strawberries. They ate what they could and then filled a twelve-quart water bucket. These berries furnished them and the families who entertained them with a real treat during their three-day visit.

The weekend meetings were held in the Chapman home.

The family invited their neighbors to attend, but only one family ventured to come. Many people were prejudiced against the Adventists because of the disappointment of 1844.

As Loughborough and Cornell visited groups of Adventists they found the people would sometimes advertise a grove meeting and would arrange log or plank seats under the trees. After one of these two-day meetings eight persons were baptized. The congregation had been dismissed and the ministers were on their way back to the house where they were staying, when one of the persons who had been at the service stepped up to the ministers and said, "I cannot let you brethren leave without taking my stand for the truth. Will you come back to the stream and baptize me?" So John Loughborough returned with the candidate, and, as the sun was sinking out of sight, the two men went down into the water. To the convert who was beginning a new life of faith and obedience, Loughborough said, "Such an experience as this repays us well for all our long, wearisome journeys, away from loved ones and friends, with weeks sometimes passing without any letters from home."

One day, at the close of the meeting, a man came to the ministers with the request: "My little ten-year-old boy is sick at home with a severe fever; will you come home with me? He says that if you will come and pray for him he is sure he will get well."

After a moment's thought Mr. Loughborough answered, "We would be glad to come and pray for him; but if we go to your house, it will mean several miles of extra driving, and I am afraid that would make us so late that we could not reach our next stopping place before dark, and we might get lost." So the two men got into their carriage and started on their way. Imagine their surprise when, after an hour's ride, they found the road closed by a gate. Opening it, they passed through and found themselves in a yard.

The man who had invited them to come to his home rushed out of the house, exclaiming, "We are so happy you came!"

The two ministers had been so deeply interested talking together as they rode along that they did not notice when the horse turned off the main road and trotted toward the home where the sick boy lived. The ministers engaged in prayer for the youth, and the Lord healed him. The fever left, and he arose and went about the house as well as ever. In spite of the seeming delay the two men reached their stopping place before dark.

Strangers found it almost impossible to travel over the prairies at night. Often the roads were mere tracks, with no fences or signposts to guide travelers. Sometimes wagon trails crossed the road or branched out in many directions. Even if there had been signposts, the travelers could not have read them without getting out of the carriage and deciphering them by the dim light of kerosene lanterns. Road maps, if there had been any, would have helped little.

When asking directions, the travelers would be pointed to some distant landmark—perhaps a clump of trees, a windmill, a barn, or a group of houses. They would be told to keep their eyes on the object in view and to drive straight toward it. When they reached that point they would inquire again and be directed to another landmark. On reaching their destination the men would inquire of the first person they met for the family they wished to visit.

In those days the only literature on the advent message consisted of a few small tracts; a little book by Mrs. White called *Christian Experience and Views; The Youth's Instructor,* which was issued once a month, with four Sabbath-school lessons and several articles in each number; and the *Review and Herald,* published every two weeks in Rochester, New York, and sent out free of charge to those who had no money to pay for it.

For months these two earnest gospel messengers traveled from farm to farm and from settlement to settlement in Illinois and Wisconsin, seeking for those who believed in Christ's coming. They were encouraged to hold fast to God's promises and to prepare to meet their Saviour. The ministers also instructed the people in the third angel's message.

In September the itinerating ministers were nearing the end of their journey when, in alighting from the carriage, John Loughborough struck his finger against the iron tire of the wheel. This produced a painful felon on the bone which swelled up to three times its normal size, and his arm swelled to the shoulder.

When the gospel messengers, Loughborough and Cornell, reached Plymouth, their journey's end, where they were to deliver up the horse and carriage, John found a letter from his wife, who was at Olcott, New York. In it she expressed the hope that he would be able to come to her. She was studying the Bible with the Woodhull family, old friends with whom she and Mrs. Orton had been visiting, and who were ready to begin keeping the Sabbath. In harmony with his wife's request he met her at Lockport, and together they went to Olcott.

7–L.G.F.

When they reached the place, the two women suggested a Bible study for the next evening; but he said, "I have had no sleep for two nights, because of the terrible pain in this felon."

Mrs. Woodhull replied, "Give out the appointment. We will pray, and the Lord will heal your felon." So they made the appointment, and before time for the evening meeting the pain ceased, the swelling disappeared, and the core came out of the felon. Mr. Loughborough was ready to give the Bible study.

Mary Loughborough told her husband an interesting experience she had had with Mrs. Woodhull. One morning after breakfast the woman had said, "If this is all true that you have been telling us, and this is really the last message, why is there not someone having visions? According to the prophecy of Joel, before the end people will have visions."

Mary had the book, *Christian Experience and Views*, with her, which told of the wonderful way in which God had spoken to His people through Ellen G. White. Mrs. Loughborough handed her the book, saying, "Sister Woodhull, you take this book and read it. We will do your morning's work while you read the book." The woman sat down in another room to read. She would read and wipe the tears from her eyes. She finished reading the book before she said a word. Then she announced, "That settles it; I am satisfied now. I shall keep the Sabbath." She and her husband lived to be more than seventy years old, and they kept God's Sabbath to the end of their lives.

While at Olcott, John Loughborough held several evening meetings in the Wesleyan chapel. In the audience were Mr. and Mrs. Lindsay and Letha Ann Whiting and her mother, who was the granddaughter of Cotton Mather of Boston. These four persons took their stand for the Sabbath. At first Mrs. Lindsay was much troubled. She said, "What can we do? We have always taught our children to keep Sunday. How can we lead them to keep another day?"

Mr. Loughborough was startled to hear himself say, "Never mind about the children. Do your duty and the Lord will bring your children to keep the Sabbath."

"We will obey and trust the Lord," said the woman.

When Mr. Loughborough returned to Olcott a few weeks later, he found the younger children keeping the Sabbath with their parents. However, the two older ones, Harmon and Mary, were bitter against the new religious views. At the close of the first meeting Mrs. Lindsay came to John Loughborough with tears in her eyes, saying, "You said the Lord would bring the children into this truth. Mary says, 'If Loughborough comes to this house I will turn him out of doors.'"

"Never mind, they are alive yet," the minister said comfortingly. "I think I had better go home to dinner with you."

Mary Lindsay was surprised at the pleasant way in which the Adventist minister greeted her. Soon after this the young woman attended a Wesleyan revival and was converted. When the minister asked if she would like to join the church, she said, "No, the seventh day is the Sabbath, and I shall unite with the Adventists." Not long afterward, Harmon Lindsay also took his stand for the Sabbath. Mary became the wife of Elijah Gaskill, one of our early colporteur evangelists to Africa, and her brother Harmon became a worker in Africa and in New England.

During the summer of 1853 John Loughborough held

meetings in New York State in several large communities.

In November the Loughboroughs went to Ohio, where a Sabbathkeeping family gave the couple a home. To this retreat John Loughborough could retire between preaching tours. During these short rest periods he wrote a fifty-two-page tract on the two-horned beast of Revelation 13. It had been two years since he first started studying this question with the Sabbathkeeping company at Rochester, New York. There he had learned that this two-horned beast represented a power which would appear in the last days and would attempt to compel the whole world to worship the first beast.

Loughborough had planned to remain with the Ohio believers only a month; but the interest was so great he could not get away until May, 1854. During his ministry in the state the number of Sabbathkeepers there was more than doubled.

Early in May, 1854, Elder and Mrs. James White met Joseph Bates and John Loughborough in Milan, Ohio, where a conference was scheduled. About forty Sabbathkeeping brethren were in attendance, and Elder White could write, "Ohio is now a promising field," as the result of the meetings held the previous months.

The workers traveled to Michigan, where they were joined by Elder Cornell. The first meetings were held in Jackson and Locke. On Sunday the house was packed. The ministers scarcely knew what to do with such a large congregation, until someone suggested that a window be taken out so an opening could be made in the wall. This was done, and with an improvised pulpit at the opening, the speakers could be heard by those seated inside the building and also by many persons sitting on the grass and in their carriages outside.

The next day, as the brethren were traveling to an appointment at Sylvan, they discussed the problem of finding proper meeting places to accommodate the crowds that were now coming to hear the message.

"In the summer we can hold grove meetings," volunteered Elder White, adding, as an afterthought, "but, of course, it might rain."

Someone suggested using tents. "That's a good idea," said Mrs. White.

Elder White's next comment was, "Perhaps by another season we can start the tents."

"Why not have a tent at once?" ventured Cornell.

The more the subject was considered, the more determined were the leaders for immediate action. The next question was where they could get the money to buy the tent. Finally it was decided to pray over the matter, and discuss it with the brethren at Sylvan and Jackson. When they arrived at the home of C. S. Glover in Sylvan, Elder White told him about the large crowd that came to the meeting at Locke. "The time has come when people are interested to hear the message, and we must find places that will accommodate the crowds," he said. "What do you think, Brother Glover, about our buying a large tent for the meetings in Michigan this summer?"

Glover inquired as to the cost of such a tent. When told it would be about $200, the brother left the room and soon returned, holding in his hand $35 in gold and silver coins. He handed this money to Elder White, saying as he did so, "There is what I think of it. I will venture that much on it."

At Jackson they visited J. P. Kellogg, who listened to what Elder White had to say, and then asked, "How much do you think such a tent would cost?" He was told that $200 should purchase the tent and equipment. Then Mr. Kellogg did exactly what Mr. Glover had done. He excused himself and returned with $35. Handing the money to Elder White, Kellogg said, "That is what I think about it. Now you had better see Brethren Palmer and Smith. Whatever more you need to make up the $200, I will let you have it, until you can raise it from the brethren."

About noon the next day, Elder Cornell left the house where the group were visiting with the Palmer family, and, with the $200 in hand, boarded the train for Detroit to purchase the tent.

That same evening Elder and Mrs. White left for Wisconsin to attend meetings. As the time drew near for them to take the train, they joined their friends in a season of prayer for God's protection on the journey. At eight o'clock John Loughborough walked down to the station with the Whites to help carry their luggage and assist them to their seats. They entered a car called the sleeping car, because it had high-backed seats that could be pushed into a reclining position.

As Mrs. White sat down she said, "James, I can't stay in this car. I must get out of here." John helped them move into the next car on the train. Again she seemed uneasy. "I don't feel at home on this train," she said. The car bell rang. John bade them good-by, left the train, and walked back to the home of Cyrenius Smith, where he was staying.

As he was getting to sleep about ten o'clock he heard someone knocking at the front door, and who should it be but Elder White. He brought them the disquieting word that the train had been wrecked about three miles from Jackson. Abram Dodge, a son-in-law to Smith, soon had the horse and carriage ready, and they went with Elder White to get Mrs. White. After doing what little he could to help the injured, Elder White had carried his wife across swampy land to the main road, where he had found a house. Here Mrs. White had remained while her husband rode into Jackson with the messenger sent for physicians to care for the injured.

The story, as the Whites recounted it, is as follows: "The train had run about three miles from Jackson when its motion became very violent, jerking backward and forward, and finally stopping. I opened the window and saw one car raised nearly upon end. I heard agonizing groans, and there was great confusion. The engine had been thrown from the track, but the car we were in was on the track, and was separated about one hundred feet from those before it. The coupling had not been broken, but our car had been unfastened from the one before it, as if an angel had separated them. The baggage car was not much injured, and our large trunk of books was uninjured. The second-class car was crushed, and the pieces, with the passengers, were thrown on both sides of the track. The car in which we had tried to get a seat was much broken, and one end was raised upon the heap of ruins. Four were killed or mortally wounded, and many were much injured. We could but feel that God had sent an angel to preserve our lives."—*Life Sketches,* pages 153, 154.

In the morning Loughborough and the other men went to look over the wreck. It was at a point where a road crossed the track. As the train came around a curve, the engineer had seen an ox lying in the road, directly on the track between the rails. Before he could stop the train, the engine struck the animal, throwing the engine and cab off the track. The baggage car jumped the tracks, but was uninjured. In it was a trunk of tracts and papers, including many copies of Elder White's new tract, *The Signs of the Times*, and Mrs. White's book, *Christian Experience and Views*, which they were taking to distribute among the church members. Neither the trunk nor its contents were injured.

The engine had run a few rods along the side of the track and, after starting to climb a sandbank, had struck a large oak stump and turned upside down directly across the track. The following cars had jammed into the engine and were smashed. A car with eighteen passengers was wrecked, and one passenger in it was killed. The third car was the one in which the Whites had first taken seats. It was badly damaged, and the seats where Elder White and his wife had been sitting before they changed to the rear car, were completely crushed. The rear car, in which the Whites were riding, had been disconnected from the rest of the train, and stood on the track almost a hundred feet from the wreck.

In relating this experience, Loughborough said, "As we viewed the wreck, and then the car in which Elder White and his wife were riding at the time of the accident, standing quietly by itself, . . . we felt to say in our hearts, God heard prayer, and who knows but He sent his angel to uncouple that car, that His servants might escape unharmed? More especially did this thought impress our minds when the brakeman said that he did not uncouple it, and furthermore, that no one was on the platform when it occurred, and that it was a mystery to him and all the trainmen how it was done; and what was still more mysterious to them, the link and bolt were both unbroken, and the bolt with its chain was lying on the platform of the wrecked car as though placed there by a careful hand."

Only a few hours were required for the workmen to clear the wreckage from the railroad track, and on the evening of May 24 another train left for Chicago at the regular hour. With a delay of only twenty-four hours Elder and Mrs. White went on their way.

Where was Elder Cornell and what was he doing in the meantime? The tent he had thought to secure in Detroit was already sold, so he went on to Rochester, New York, to see Mr. Williams, who had made tents for Adventists in 1844. For only $160 Williams sold him a strong sixty-foot circular tent which had been used only a few days. He threw into the bargain a fifteen-foot duck flag bearing the motto, "What Is Truth?"

Within two weeks from the time that the idea of a tent was first mentioned, the tent had been purchased and paid for, and a vacant lot had been secured in Battle Creek on which to pitch it. On June 10, Elder Loughborough saw the tent, with seats and lighting fixtures, ready for the opening meeting, in which the subject of Daniel 2 was presented.

Earlier in the day, while the work of preparation was going on, the postmaster of Battle Creek came over to see what kind of show had come to town. After some conversation with the ministers he went back and told everyone he saw to attend the meetings and hear something worth while.

PUBLIC EVANGELISM ADVANCES

15

THE first two meetings in the new tent were a success. John Loughborough wrote in the *Review and Herald,* July 4, 1854: "Our meetings were well attended. . . . It was estimated by several that on Sunday evening there were not less than one thousand people on the ground."

Where should the next meeting be held? The workers gathered at the home of one of the brethren to pray for guidance. When they arose, Elder White said, "In my judgment, the time has come for Brother John to be ordained to the work of the ministry. If you brethren are of the same mind, we will have the ordination ceremony tonight." They knelt down again, and Elders White and Cornell laid their hands on the head of the young minister, now only twenty-two years old, and prayed that the Lord would spare his life, bless his labors, and enable him to bring many souls to the kingdom.

John Loughborough was among the first to be ordained as a minister in what was later known as the Seventh-day Adventist denomination. The other ministers engaged in the work at that time had been ordained in other denominations before joining the Adventists.

Public Evangelism Advances

During that summer tent meetings had been held in many towns in Michigan. On a Friday afternoon the big tent would go up, two meetings would be held Sabbath and three on Sunday. Then the tent would be taken down on Monday and loaded on a wagon, and the two ministers and the tent master would travel to the next town selected for meetings. Where there was a special interest, the speakers might continue their meetings for a week or longer.

Storms sometimes hindered the meetings. At Saline, Michigan, the series of sermons began unfavorably. Elder Loughborough writes, "We pitched our tent on sixth-day (Friday), and in the p.m. a sudden gale arose and the wind blew with such violence as to tear down the tent, breaking the center pole and several hooks and ropes, in consequence of which we were obliged to meet on the Sabbath in the village schoolhouse." But the men had the tent up Sunday morning ready for a full week of meetings!

When harvesttime came, the farmers were busy gathering in their hay and grain. The tent was erected in a grove, and meetings were conducted for three weeks. Every Sunday night, after the last preaching service, the tent would be quickly lowered, rolled up, and stored until the following Friday afternoon; and early Monday morning Elders Loughborough and Cornell and their tent master would be off to work in the harvest fields. During these three weeks, the three men earned about $40. They pooled their earnings; and after paying what was still lacking on the expenses of the meetings, they had some left to send their families.

In those days there was no tithing system, and the workers received no dependable wages. Occasionally a call for funds to help some especially needy enterprise would be made through the *Review and Herald.* When there was sufficient money in the tent fund, the workers would allow themselves a wage of three or four dollars a week to help in their living expense. Collections were sometimes taken up, but usually the only contributions came from generous-hearted listeners, who, at the close of the meetings, would give the ministers fifty cents or a dollar. The tracts and periodicals were given away, and the printing was paid for by personal gifts. For this reason there was never enough money at the printing office in Rochester, New York, to publish all the literature needed.

One day sometime previously, while discussing ways and means of advancing the gospel work, Elder White said, "I think, Brother John, that if our books were offered to the public in connection with our preaching, the people would be willing to buy, and to pay a small price for them, and that would enable us to publish much more literature than we are now doing."

The alert young preacher answered, "I will try it." So at one meeting the tracts were displayed on the speaker's stand and offered for sale. At the close of the sermon many persons came forward and purchased them. At that time a complete set of all Adventist literature published including tracts and one paper-covered book, could be purchased for thirty-five cents. One man laid down an extra coin, after paying for his tracts, stating that he was making a contribution to help defray the expenses of the tent. Others followed his example, and when the ministers counted the money, they found they had $18.

The report of these first tent-meeting sales was printed in

the *Review and Herald,* and other ministers began to sell literature in connection with their evangelistic meetings. The money was sent to the printing office, and new tracts and books were published with the contributions. Soon after this a call was made for a tract fund to supply the ministers with tracts to give out freely.

One Sunday after a sermon on the Sabbath question some of the people said they would like to hear *their* minister give *his* views on the subject. So Elder Cornell called on the minister and invited him to speak in the tent the next Sunday. He said, "We have been telling the people that Saturday the seventh day is the Sabbath, and now we would like to have you tell us what you believe."

On the following Sunday morning every seat in the tent was occupied and many people were sitting on the grass under the trees outside. There were 246 farm wagons that had carried entire families, and, in addition, many had walked or come on horseback. The minister who had been invited to present his ideas on Sundaykeeping was there at nine o'clock in time to hear Elder Loughborough present a message on the law of God.

When the minister opposing the Sabbath arose to speak, he seemed confused. He passed rapidly over his remarks on the law, turning two or three pages of his sermon notes at a time. Then he read several quotations from the fathers of the Catholic Church, giving the reasons why the early Christian church ceased to observe the "old Jewish Sabbath" and, in its place, honored Sunday.

After the man sat down, Elder Loughborough announced that he would review his sermon at one o'clock. He invited all the congregation, and especially the minister himself, to stay; but the minister refused to remain, although some of his church members begged him to do so. During the lunch hour a member of the congregation who had heard the morning talk, said to Elder Loughborough, "You have been telling us about Sundaykeeping being founded on tradition and not upon the authority of the Scriptures, and our minister seems to agree with you on this point."

Long before one o'clock the tent was again crowded, and some were sitting on the grass outside. Elder Loughborough briefly reviewed the remarks of the visiting minister, and then preached a sermon on the third angel's message, with its earnest warning against worshiping the beast and his image. He called attention to the historic facts which had already been presented that morning by their guest speaker, and showed that these facts proved that human beings had tried to interfere with the government of God, and to change His law, by substituting another rest day for the one God had appointed, and by commanding the church to observe this man-made sabbath.

Many of those present expressed their determination to be loyal to the God of heaven and to keep His commandments. Another minister named Lawrence was in the audience that day. He had come in the hope of strengthening his arguments for Sundaykeeping. As he rode home that afternoon, some of his companions who had accompanied him asked, "Pastor Lawrence, what do you think of this day's talk?" Putting his hand to his head, he said, "Oh, my head is so full, I shall have to take three weeks to think it out." He did think it out, and he studied the Scriptures. As a result he spent the rest of his life preaching the truths of the coming of Jesus, the judgment, and God's law.

Public Evangelism Advances 105

By midsummer of 1855 there were in various states of the Union five large tents, each requiring the services of two ministers and a tent master to conduct meetings. In the fall, when cold weather came on, the tents were rolled up and stored in barn lofts until the following spring. Whenever the workers could earn some money on weekdays, they would put their earnings together in a common fund and draw from it for personal expenses.

Much prayer and faith were needed by the ministers and their patient, self-sacrificing wives and children at home. They often skimped and sacrificed in order to make the few dollars their husbands were able to send them go as far as possible in supplying the bare necessities of life.

In the summer of 1856 Elder Loughborough was feeling discouraged, wondering how he was going to provide for himself and his wife during the coming winter. He received a letter from John Andrews, who, with his father's family and some others, had moved to Waukon, Iowa. A company of about thirty had secured land and were beginning to build homes in the Midwest state. They were planning to raise grain and other crops while they brought the message to the settlers in the community. This letter from his old friend made Loughborough and his wife decide that this was a way to secure a cheap home where he could work to support his family.

Imagine their disappointment when, on reaching the place, they found that Waukon was only a small village, surrounded by open prairie, with a few farmhouses scattered here and there, affording him little opportunity for preaching. Soon after the Loughboroughs arrived, a heavy snow covered the ground to a depth of a foot or more. This was followed by a thaw, then sleet; another freeze, more snow, another thaw and a freeze. Within a few days the ground was covered with three layers of ice with snow sandwiched in between. The little town of Waukon was completely snowed in! It was almost impossible to go anywhere, because the horses would break through the thin crusts of ice at almost every step. Elder Loughborough bought himself a set of carpenter tools and went to work to earn money to buy food and clothing and to build a house.

He had worked at his trade only a few weeks, when one day as he and Mr. Mead were hammering away on a store building, they heard someone call to them, "That sounds like Elon Everts's voice," said Mead; and it was.

"Come down," he called. "Brother and Sister White and Brother Hart are out here in a sleigh."

John Loughborough guessed what they had come for, and his pleasure at seeing them was somewhat mingled with apprehension. Soon he was standing beside the sleigh, and Mrs. White said in a solemn voice, "What doest thou here, Elijah?" Three times she asked this question without saying another word. He did not know what to answer. At first he felt embarrassed that she should compare him with the prophet Elijah. On second thought, he remembered that Elijah had once become discouraged, and had run away. Now he, John Loughborough, was trying to run away from duty and seclude himself in this little village.

How could these friends have reached Waukon through the deep snows? The last he had heard of them they were holding meetings at Round Grove, Illinois about fifty miles away. The story of that journey they were to hear later from the lips of Mrs. White.

Public Evangelism Advances

Why had these messengers come so far through cold and snow over dangerous roads? It was because the Lord had shown Mrs. White that the company at Waukon needed help. She was greatly troubled by the vision. "James," she said to her husband, "we must go and visit our brethren in Waukon." They talked the matter over with two of their friends, Josiah Hart and Elon Everts, and decided to make the trip with two horses and a sleigh.

Then something happened that threatened to spoil their plans; the rain came pouring down and melted the snow. Elder White thought they would have to give up the trip. Hart asked, "Sister White, what about Waukon?"

She answered, "We shall go."

"Yes," he replied, "if God works a miracle!"

Many times that night she was up, looking out of the window. About daybreak a change came in the weather, and the rain turned to snow. By five o'clock that night the snow was deep enough to make sleighing possible, and at once the four started on their long, cold journey. While waiting for a blizzard to pass, they stopped at Green Vale and held meetings with the Sabbathkeepers there for nearly a week. Then, as the weather cleared, they resumed their journey.

One night, weary, cold, and hungry, the group stopped at a hotel a few miles from the Mississippi River. The next morning about four o'clock it began to rain, but they felt urged to go on. At nearly every step the horses broke through the crusted snow. The travelers knew that there was no bridge across the river. In summer the wagons and carriages were ferried over, and in winter sleighs crossed on the ice. Hart inquired of several people along the way, and always received the same answer: "It would be dangerous to try to cross." They informed him that the ice over the river was spongy and mixed with snow, and that there was a foot of water on top of it. Several teams had broken through the ice and the drivers barely escaped with their lives.

As they neared the river, Hart stood up in the sleigh, and asked, "Is it Iowa or back to Illinois? We have come to the Red Sea. Shall we cross?" The answer came back, "Go forward, trusting in Israel's God." They drove carefully onto the ice, praying as they went. It held firm. As the sleigh ascended the Iowa bank of the river, the group in the sleigh bowed their heads and offered a prayer of thanksgiving.

It was Friday afternoon, so the party stopped at a hotel in Dubuque to rest over the Sabbath. In the evening they gathered in the parlor and sang hymns. Then Hart hung up his chart and gave a Bible study. "Call on us again on your way back," said the proprietor, "and we will assure you a good congregation."

Sunday morning the travelers faced the cold again, which grew colder and colder. Occasionally some member of the group would call out, "Brother, your face is freezing, you'd better rub the frost out of it as soon as possible." Then it would be, "Your ear is freezing," or, "Your nose is freezing." As they neared Waukon they prayed more earnestly than ever that God would bless their visit to the little company.

It was the night before Christmas when the families met in the Andrews home. Meetings were held every night from December 24 to 31. At one of these meetings Mrs. White was given a vision, in which she was shown some things regarding those present. When they first went to Iowa, it

Public Evangelism Advances

was with the intention of answering a call made through the *Review*, for some Sabbathkeepers to go West "to do good to souls, to live out their faith, and tell those around them that this world is not their home." They had failed to do this; they were losing their first love and were growing lukewarm. Working early and late in their efforts to earn money, there was little time left for them to talk with their neighbors about the love of Jesus and His soon coming. Within the group faultfinding and criticism and bitter feelings arose. God's message to them was, "Return, ye backsliding children, and I will heal your backslidings."

The Spirit of Jesus came into the meeting. James White declared: "These meetings were the most powerful we had witnessed for years." Mrs. Loughborough stood up and confessed her own lack of consecration. She pleaded with her husband, "Go forth in the name of the Lord to do His work."

Elder Loughborough cried out, "I have laid up my hammer and driven the last nail."

One brother had been buying land as fast as he could in the hope of getting rich. To this brother, Mrs. White said, "Now you have a chance to redeem the past; you can take Brother Loughborough back with you to labor in Illinois, and care for him there."

"I will do it," said the man.

When the visiting group returned to Illinois, John Loughborough went back with them to join Everts and Hart in their labor. His chief thoughts now were not of himself and the difficulties he must face. The picture of his brave, young wife, smiling through her tears as she waved him good-by, would not fade from his mind. She had remained behind without knowing when she would see him again. She was willing to endure the privations and hardships of a cold winter in that pioneer country without the strong help of her companion. From that memorable day in Waukon, until the day of her death, Mary Loughborough valiantly and lovingly shared her husband's labors and oftentimes his travels. When unable to go with him, her regular attendance at the prayer meeting and her fervent testimonies and prayers cheered the hearts of the advent believers.

At the request of the man who had been buying land, the travelers stopped at a store and gave him a chance to start carrying out his commission. He bought a buffalo robe and some flannel cloth. As he climbed back into the sleigh, he said, "Elder, I am going to ask Sister Lockwood to make this material into a warm buffalo overcoat for you."

Soon after this, John Andrews left his farming and went to preach again. Others of the Waukon group followed. Two great men had been saved to the work of God, and never again did they entertain any temptation to leave it.

At the time of the Waukon meetings a young man who considered himself a sort of infidel was away from home on a Mississippi River boat. While the boat was docked, waiting for the ice to melt, he went ashore. There the Spirit of God spoke to his heart, saying, "Believe the Bible; accept it as the word of God." He answered, "Yes, Lord, I will." He returned to the boat, went to his cabin, and there, on his knees, gave himself to God. When he returned to Waukon and heard the story of what had taken place there during his absence he dedicated his life to the service of God. That young man was George I. Butler, who later served for nearly eleven years as president of the General Conference.

BRIGHTER DAYS

16

BRIGHTER days were ahead for John Loughborough, but they were not yet visible. For the remaining three winter months, while traveling and preaching most of the time, he received ten dollars in cash for his labors. In addition to this he received free board and room from the families he visited. In April he returned to Waukon to see his wife, walking twenty-six miles of the journey with a heavy satchel on his back, that he might save his fare and have a little money to give her when he reached home. During the four summer months he held meetings in Wisconsin and Illinois and received twenty dollars in addition to his board and traveling expenses.

The other ministers throughout the field were also working for meager compensation. Though they were perplexed at times they were happy in doing the Lord's work. They realized that the benefits received were only a small part of their real wages—the greater part would be given them in the day of final rewards.

By this time the *Review and Herald* office had been moved from Rochester, New York, to Battle Creek, Michigan. In the new building, a steam power press was turning out thousands of pages of tracts and papers every week. The *Review and Herald* was now being printed regularly; and the list of subscribers who were able to pay for their paper was growing, while the "worthy poor," who received it free, was diminishing. *The Youth's Instructor* could be obtained for twenty-five cents a year; but a special appeal was made for all who "choose to pay fifty cents," to do so.

New tracts, written by the ministers, were printed as rapidly as possible. These were sent out to be sold or distributed free of charge by those who were holding public meetings. Where did the money come from to do all this? It was raised by freewill offerings. Church members, in the warmth of their new love, and their consuming zeal to spread the knowledge of Christ's soon coming, deprived themselves of every unnecessary pleasure and luxury. They worked and planned and economized in order to have a few dollars to send to the *Review and Herald* offices to help the work along. Prosperous merchants and mechanics could do more. The farmers were having a hard time to get cash. Crops had been abundant, but prices were low, causing a scarcity of money. In spite of this many gave generously. Two men, J. P. Kellogg and Henry Lyon, sold their valuable farms and contributed hundreds of dollars toward the erection of an office building and the purchase of machinery.

The winters of 1856 and 1857 were hard on all the workers, especially the traveling ministers. Many times the freewill offerings they received from the churches they visited scarcely paid their traveling expenses, and there was often little or nothing left for them to send to their families.

For some months Elder White was kept so busy at the office that he had little time for traveling. He arranged for

Brighter Days 113

Elder Loughborough to use his horse and buggy when visiting churches in Michigan. He also raised money to help him buy a small house in Battle Creek. The conscientious minister always considered this money a loan, and he returned it later by investing it in the Lord's work. The young couple moved from Iowa to Battle Creek in the autumn of 1857, happy that they could be together in a home of their own.

Mary set about taking in boarders to help supplement the family income. Her husband's wages in cash for the first winter's work after moving to Battle Creek amounted to only four dollars. In addition to this the farmers helped supply their table, with ten bushels of wheat, five bushels of apples, five bushels of potatoes, a peck of beans, thirty pounds of maple sugar—yes, and there was a ham and half a hog! This was several years before Seventh-day Adventists discarded swine's flesh as food, for it was not until 1863 that Mrs. White was given a vision concerning healthful living and was especially warned against the use of pork and other diseased flesh foods.

On January 16, 1859, the church members in Battle Creek came together for an important meeting. They met in the new church, a plain wooden building, 28 x 42 feet in size, to try to find some plan for supporting the ministers. After much study a plan was suggested that seemed to be a good one, because it gave all the members a part in helping, some more, some less, according as they were able. The plan was for each brother between the ages of eighteen and sixty to lay away on the first day of the week from five to twenty-five cents, and each sister from two to ten cents, according as God had prospered them. Those who owned houses and farms were asked to give every week from one to five cents on every hundred dollars' worth of property. This plan of giving, called *systematic benevolence*, was adopted January 26, 1859, and was followed for a number of years until the church was ready to accept the tithing system.

For ten years John and Mary Loughborough lived at Battle Creek. He spent much of his time visiting churches in the winter and holding tent meetings in the summer. There was always the little home on Champion Street and the wife waiting for him whenever he could be spared a few days from his public labors. After awhile there was someone else waiting for him, too, someone whom he proudly called "my son Delmer."

During the summer of 1865, Elder Loughborough labored for two months in Iowa. The strenuous labors finally made it necessary for him to retire from the work for a few months at Dansville, New York.

Of his Iowa labors he wrote, "First-day I preached twice to attentive congregations, and then returned sixteen miles to Waterloo with Brother Jackson, and had a meeting from nine o'clock p.m. till four the next morning, on matters of difficulty in the church. . . . After getting four hours sleep, I returned on Monday, sixteen miles to La Porte, and spent the evening till ten o'clock conversing with those who wished to know something of the history of the rise of the third angel's message. . . .

"Tuesday, August 8, traveled by stage thirty-five miles over very bad roads to Blairstown, where I found I must remain till the next morning before I could take the cars. Here I had no place to stop but a small country tavern, and that was nearly filled with drunken hogdrovers. They caroused all night and had three regular fist fights before midnight. I got no rest of any consequence that night. The next morning, took the cars and rode seventy-five miles to Nevada. Here I found no food fit for a human being to eat, but I did the best I could, and started on for Fort Des Moines, by stage thirty-five miles. It was one o'clock the next night before I reached that place. The roads were in such a terrible state that it took us five hours to accomplish the first ten miles of the journey; and all the stages on the route that day were finally abandoned, and the passengers taken through by private conveyance. The next morning I arose at seven, and tried to make out a breakfast at the Western Tavern, where hog's grease was the predominating article.

"From that place I went twenty-two miles to Sandyville, by private conveyance, during which time the weather was so hot that the horses could not be driven faster than a walk, and it took till four o'clock p.m. to complete the journey. At Sandyville I fortunately got a little rest before the meeting." The letter gave other details, and ends thus:

"In my reduced condition of health I rode that afternoon fourteen miles on my way to Pella. Had another chill on the way. Stopped at a crowded hotel and got a little rest. In the morning took cars twenty-six miles to Eddyville, expecting to preach a funeral sermon there, and attend a business meeting that day; but as I stepped off the cars, Brother John Kirfman handed me the *Review*, in which was the account of the sickness of Brother White, and a call for me to come home. I immediately decided to go, and stepping back upon the same train, I came on to Battle Creek, five hundred and sixty-two miles."

In those days when the whereabouts of traveling brethren was uncertain, the *Review and Herald,* which was sent out to all church members, was often the quickest means of contacting workers and making appointments.

While the conductor held the train, Elder Loughborough read the account of Elder White's illness, and the notice to him personally, which said, "Brother Loughborough's appointment at Liberty, Iowa, August 26 and 27, is taken up in consequence of his being sent for to come to Battle Creek, on account of the sudden sickness of Brother White. Brother L. is requested to come *immediately.*"

Dr. H. S. Lay was at the station in Battle Creek to meet Elder Loughborough on his arrival. He advised that Elder White be taken at once to a health retreat conducted in Dansville, New York. Here he could rest from his travels and his labors. He would receive good treatment every day with hot and cold water, and he would have regular meals and plenty of rest. Dr. Lay had visited this institution, "Our Home on the Hillside," as it was called, and he considered it to be the best place for the patient.

The doctor also gave Elder Loughborough a physical checkup and advised him to go along with Elder White and have a good rest himself. The poor man was suffering such pain in his head that much of the time he walked on tiptoe to save the jarring caused by ordinary walking. When the minister remarked that they had been trying to live by the rules of health, the doctor reminded him that there was one rule which they all had neglected: a regular time for rest and sleep. Elder and Mrs. White and Elder Loughborough had traveled much together. After a long journey on the train or in a carriage or stagecoach, they would frequently reach their destination just in time to go to a meeting, with not a moment to rest. After the meeting, their time was taken up in visiting. At night, while the family who were entertaining them slept, the ministers often sat up writing articles or letters by candlelight or by a dim kerosene lamp, while Mrs. White wrote out the messages the Lord had given her for various individuals.

After six weeks at "Our Home on the Hillside" Elder Loughborough was sufficiently recovered to take Elder and Mrs. White out riding every day in a borrowed carriage. As Elder White was too weak to walk up the hill to the dining room, John would bring the sick man's dinner to his room in the cottage. They remained at the retreat for another six weeks; but it was almost two years before Elder White had recovered sufficiently from the stroke of paralysis to take up his work again.

A few years after this, Elder Loughborough took a one-year medical course. Then he wrote a book called *Handbook of Health*. It was a small treatise on physiology and hygiene, cheap enough for every family to own a copy, and simple enough for them to read and understand.

WESTWARD TO CALIFORNIA

17

"HAS no one any impressions of duty relative to the California field?" asked James White at the sixth annual session of the General Conference of Seventh-day Adventists, which opened at Battle Creek, May 12, 1868, with two hundred fifty ministers and workers in attendance. Elder John N. Andrews, who was president of the General Conference that year, had been calling on the various ministers to state the particular field where they felt impressed that the Lord would have them labor during the coming year.

Merritt G. Kellogg, later a physician, was attending the conference for the first time. For almost nine years he and his family had been in California. The story of their trek overland in a covered wagon, through wolf- and snake-infested country, over mountain trails and across sunburnt deserts; their experiences with broken bones and broken wagon wheel, worn-out shoes and bruised feet, hailstorms, near starvation and water shortage, fear of Indians and drunken drivers—all make a thrilling tale, as related by Dr. H. O. McCumber in his book, *Pioneering the Message in the Golden West*. But it was not of these things that Kellogg

Westward to California 119

told the brethren at the conference. It was the news that thousands of gold seekers were rushing out to California with the dream of becoming rich. These people needed to be reminded of the heavenly riches. Could not the conference send workers to start a mission in California?

Kellogg told them that he had found a few people who had become interested in studying present truth by reading tracts and papers sent them through the mail. He had been meeting every Sabbath with a group in the home of a B. G. St. John, a lumber tallyman at the wharves. There was also J. W. Cronkrite, who had come from the East to set up a shoe-repair shop in San Francisco. Back of his cobbler's bench he hung a prophetic chart and the Ten Commandment chart. By study of the Scriptures he had prepared himself to answer any questions that his customers might ask about these charts while they were having measurements taken for a pair of shoes or while waiting for old ones to be repaired. The believers in California were doing what they could, Kellogg told the brethren; but they needed a minister to conduct public meetings.

For months Elder Loughborough had been thinking about going to California. In the daytime he thought about California, and at night he dreamed of the West. He believed that God was leading him to consider laboring in that field. When Elder White asked for someone who would go to California, John arose and said that he felt impressed that God was calling him to go. There were expressions of thankfulness in many parts of the room—thankfulness that someone had volunteered to go to that "faraway" mission field.

Again Elder White spoke, "When the Lord sent forth His servants, He sent them two and two, and it seems as if there should be two to go together to this distant field. Is there no other one whose mind has been led to that field?"

D. T. Bourdeau stood up and said that he would be free to go with Elder Loughborough. "For some time," he said, "I have been impressed that God was going to send me to some faraway place. Before Mrs. Bourdeau and I came to the conference, we sold our horse and carriage, our household goods, and everything we owned, and now we are ready to go wherever the General Conference sends us."

The conference was asked to pray about the California mission, and the two ministers were urged to "be sure of the mind of the Lord." On the last day of May, as the *Review and Herald* was going to press, Elder White sat down and wrote this notice for the paper:

"After much prayer and counseling with fellow laborers, Elders Loughborough and Bourdeau decide to leave in a short time on a mission to California. They now design to take with them a new tent, in which they can hold meetings in that climate eight or nine months in the year." Elder White also appealed for $1,000, with which to pay the traveling expenses of the missionaries and to purchase the tent.

The Loughboroughs and Bourdeaus sailed from New York June 24, 1868, on a small steamer, the "Rising Star." Delmer Loughborough was three and a half years old. His own mother, Mary, had died in Battle Creek, June 24, 1867. The boy now had a stepmother, for Loughborough had married Maggie Newman in Victor, New York, in the month of June.

While in Rochester, the ministers were advised by a friend to get their steamship tickets in New York City a few days before sailing time. There was sharp competition between the American Line and the Pacific Mail. Therefore if passengers would get the best offer from the rival companies, they could save money. The ministers followed the suggestion and obtained "a good room near the center of the ship" for $467.50 for the entire party, a saving of $212.50 over the regularly quoted fare.

A storm made the sea rough, and all portholes had to be closed tight to keep out the mountainous waves that dashed against the side of the vessel as it rolled and pitched. In their stuffy cabins the passengers were tumbled about in their bunks. How sick they were! That is all but little Delmer, who lost only one meal. He was too busy trotting around looking at the strange, new things to waste time being seasick.

On shipboard were several men who were going to California to dig for gold. One of these adventurers told Elder Bourdeau that $20,000 would not tempt him to take such a trip again. The missionaries were not going to hunt for gold, but the prospect of the precious treasure they hoped to find gave them comfort and fortitude to bear cheerfully their sufferings.

After a rough voyage of ten days, the "Rising Star" docked one Friday morning at Aspinwall (now Colón), a little town on the east coast of the Isthmus of Panama. As soon as the boat stopped pitching and tossing, the sick passengers began to feel better. The missionaries gathered on deck and sang the hymns they loved, while the other passengers listened and cheered the singers.

Soon they were aboard a little train, traveling at the speed of thirteen or fourteen miles an hour. A delightful shower of rain was falling, which cooled the air and made the trip across the isthmus a pleasant one. From the car windows they could see many kinds of tropical trees that were new to them. Lemons, limes, and oranges were growing luxuriantly. Growing pineapples, bananas, mangoes, and coconuts were a thrilling sight to the strangers.

Before sundown the party were settled in their cabins on the steamer "The Golden City" and were ready for the Sabbath. The ship lay at anchor all the next day. Sunday morning the passengers were awakened by the firing of a cannon, which was the signal that in thirty minutes they would set sail for San Francisco. "The Golden City" was larger than "Rising Star." Her cabins, comfortable and roomy, were located in the center of the vessel, where the rocking motion was least felt. The Pacific was calm, and the weather warm and balmy.

The program of the day usually began and ended with a brisk walk on deck. The intervening hours were spent in visiting with fellow passengers, or in standing by the ship's rail watching the many kinds of fish, or the sea gulls that were flying about the ship looking for the scraps of food that were thrown overboard. Sometimes the attention of the voyagers was attracted by a school of porpoises racing along beside the vessel. These sea creatures, often from six to eight feet long, would jump up out of the water and then drop back into it. They swam so rapidly it seemed as though they were trying to outdistance the steamer. There were whales, sea lions, sharks, and giant turtles to interest the passengers. Sometimes schools of flying fish would rise from the water, skim along, their silver finlike wings and their scales glistening in the sunlight, and then disappear in the deep. At night it was fascinating to watch the foam in the wake of the steamer as it glowed with phosphorescent light from the bodies of sea creatures.

At ten o'clock on the following Sabbath morning, July 18, "The Golden City," docked at San Francisco. The missionary party hurried to the St. John home on Minna Street, where they found the small company of Sabbathkeepers happy to see them and glad to hear the message they brought. "Our souls were refreshed," wrote Loughborough, "as this was the first meeting which we had had the opportunity to attend since leaving Rochester."

The Loughboroughs and Bourdeaus stayed with the St. Johns, although the home was crowded. The new arrivals prepared their own meals, and they were thrilled with the variety of foods. They wrote, "It seems good indeed to be permitted to sit again at a table of fruits, grains, and vegetables. Fruits of all varieties are offered in the market here; strawberries have been in the market for the past three months. The second growth of the season is now offered. This morning we enjoyed eight pounds, which were purchased at 6¾ cents a pound, about ten cents per quart. Everything here, even to potatoes and apples, sells by the pound. In the line of fruits we now see in the market peaches of three varieties, apples of various kinds, several varieties of plums, four kinds of pears, apricots, cherries, currants, raspberries, blackberries, grapes, figs, etc. We have bought peaches here for about one dollar per bushel, and good cooking apples for the same. Apples have not been long in the market and will be cheaper soon. Grapes will soon sell for from four to five cents per pound. Of vegetables, there is every variety that any market affords.

9—L.G.F.

In addition to these, here is the finest of wheat and other grains. And if anyone wishes to regale in imported fruits, here are tropical fruits in great variety. It is strange to us to see so much fruit, and that, too, free from worm and blight. As yet, wormy fruit is unknown in this country."

The two ministers went to look for a vacant lot on which to pitch the meeting tent. They found a suitable lot in the city, but the owner wanted forty dollars a month rent for the use of it. Never before had they paid out cash for a site on which to erect a gospel tent. Prices in San Francisco seemed very high to them, and they had little money with which to begin work. They received a letter from Ellen G. White in regard to the different economic conditions in the West. Her instruction was: "You cannot labor in California as you did in New England. Such strict economy would be considered 'penny-wise' by Californians. Things are managed there on a more liberal scale. You will have to meet them in the same liberal spirit, but not in a spendthrift manner."

Thinking it might be better to start their meetings elsewhere, the men prayed earnestly that God would lead them to the right place. On July 27, a Mr. Hough, from the town of Petaluma, fifty miles to the north, called at the St. John home and invited the ministers to bring the tent to his town. He said that he belonged to a church group that called themselves "Independents." They had separated from the other churches and were studying the Bible together in an endeavor to find the truth. One of the members had received a New York newspaper through the mail which told about two ministers who were sailing for San Francisco and they were going to hold religious services in a tent. The notice had been copied as a news item from a May issue of the *Review and Herald.*

At one of the weekly prayer meetings conducted by the group, the coming of these ministers was made the subject of special prayer. On the following night, Mr. Wolf, another member of the group, dreamed of being in the open country on a dark night. He saw two men kindling a fire, and recognized them as ministers. They seemed to be building a fire, which soon burned brightly and lighted the surrounding country. Then, in his dream, he saw some men try to put the fire out by throwing brush and bunches of grass on it, which of course made it burn all the brighter. Then he saw the two ministers lighting another fire, and the enemies tried to extinguish it, too. At last they had five fires burning brightly. The man who had the dream seemed to recognize the ones who were trying to put out the fires as ministers of established churches. He heard one of them remark, "It is of no use, let them alone. The more we try to put out the fires, the brighter they burn." He also heard someone state that the ones who were lighting the fires were the two evangelists who were coming with the tent.

About that time an epidemic of smallpox struck the town. As soon as the quarantine was lifted, the Independents sent Mr. Hough to find the two evangelists who were supposed to have arrived in San Francisco. As soon as he reached the city he went at once to the Pacific Mail wharf and inquired if a tent had come from Panama on their steamer. Being informed that one had arrived, he wanted to know where it had been delivered. As he was asking the question, the drayman who had delivered the tent came into the warehouse, and he directed him to the St. John home on Minna Street.

The two missionaries thanked God for answering their prayer. The next day they went up to Petaluma to see the people who had invited them there. When Mr. Hough met them at the station, he said, "You will stop at my house tonight, but it is arranged for you to take dinner at Mr. Wolf's. I will go with you there, and come for you after dinner." Mr. Wolf had asked that the men be brought to his house, as he wanted to see them himself and be sure they were the same men he had seen in the dream. When he saw them coming with Mr. Hough he said, "Wife, *there they are;* those are the *identical* men I saw in the dream."

Soon Elders Loughborough and Bourdeau were back in San Francisco again and had the tent ready, with poles, ropes, lamps, and other fixtures. This time they took their families with them to Petaluma. The Independents took hold to help the men find a vacant lot in a quiet location. They cut stakes and helped pitch the tent. Mrs. Otis, one of the members, rented housekeeping rooms to the ministers and their families. The weather was warm, and at night the men slept in the tent.

Hough went with John Loughborough to the lumberyard to arrange for a loan of one thousand board feet of lumber, from which to make seats and a platform. Mr. Rice, the lumber dealer, looked the little minister over doubtfully, wondering if it would be safe to trust a poor preacher with such a large order. "I don't know about trusting ministers with lumber," he said dubiously. "My experience with ministers has taught me they are rather a risky set of men. At least, we've found them so here in California." Hough guaranteed that the lumber would be returned in good condition, and in a few minutes they had it loaded on the wagon.

Westward to California

On August 13, the opening night of the meeting, there were about forty persons present. It was the first public gathering in town after the smallpox epidemic. On Sunday, before the service began, the ministers laid some books and tracts on a stand in the tent. Elder Loughborough recounts what happened:

"Just before closing the service, I remarked that we had some reading matter on the subjects we were presenting. 'Here,' I stated, 'is a set of pamphlets, comprising five hundred pages, for fifty cents a package. Brother Bourdeau will give the tracts at his end of the stand to all who will receive them.' Brother Moore arose, took a package of the books, and laid down two half dollars on the stand. I said, 'We will sell them after the close of the service.' He replied, 'I was afraid I would not get any.' After the service I said to the brother, 'The books are only fifty cents.' He replied, 'A dollar is cheap enough.' As Brother Bourdeau was handing out his tracts, one man said, 'You can't afford to give away tracts for nothing. Here's a dollar. Give away a dollar's worth for me.' Another handed him fifty cents, others quarter dollars. In less time than it takes to write this, our stand was cleared of books and tracts, and the congregation was going from the tent with expressions of favor for the new ministers that had come among them." The ministers had set a price of one and two cents on the tracts; but they would have been difficult to sell at such an amount, for the smallest coin in California at the time was a ten-cent piece.

Before the second week of meetings was over another steamer had brought two more boxes of books by freight. Four shipments of books were sold at the meetings, and as orders from California continued to come into the *Review and Herald* office, Elder White wrote, "What are you doing with so many books? You are selling more books than all the tent companies east of the Rocky Mountains." At that time wages were high, money was plentiful, and books and other reading matter were scarce. The Lord had led His servants to go to California at the right time.

On the second Sunday night there were not enough seats in the tent for all who came. The sides of the tent were lifted so that those standing outside could hear. Mr. Rice, the lumber man, was present, standing by one of the side poles of the tent. As he listened intently, Elder Loughborough noticed a pleasant smile on his face. Monday morning he called on Mr. Rice at the lumberyard and said, "Mr. Rice, we need a little more lumber. You saw last night that we were short of seats."

"Elder," he replied, "you can have ten thousand feet of lumber for further seating if you want it."

Strange stories had been circulated around town about the tent company. It was reported that although one could enter free, a person would have to put money into the hat before he could get out. Naturally the people were surprised when no collection was taken and tracts were handed out free. Some of them came up front and of their own accord laid down money, saying, "We want to help with the expense of the tent."

A view of what it was like to hold tent meetings in California was reported by the evangelists in the *Review and Herald*, September 15, 1868:

"There are some pleasant features connected with tent meetings here, in contrast with tent labors in the States, to which we would call attention. We have no rain here, so everything is dry and nice as on the day we erected our tent. For this reason, a tent here, with care, will last, . . . as it will not rust out or mildew. You have not to spend an hour each day pulling at ropes, tightening and loosening to suit the weather. . . . Again our ministers know what it is to speak and sit in a damp, heavy atmosphere in the tent. There is none of it here. It is just as easy speaking in the evening in the tent as in the daytime, and we sleep in the tent with no more fear of cold than in a house. We have not here to watch the clouds for fear the people will be scared away from our meetings; we have only to watch at meeting time, and see them come in. There has been no rain of any consequence here since April. . . . No rain is expected till the middle of November. . . . A friend who has lived in this place thirteen years has just informed us he has never seen so great an interest manifested in the discussion of Bible subjects in this place before. . . . The church members in this place are some of them already alarmed to see their fellow members flocking out to see our meetings, and try to keep them away. But these Californians are too independent for the gag law, and say to them: 'Well, you may say what you please, I am going where I think best.' "

EFFORTS TO PUT OUT THE FIRE

18

THE opposition, of which Mr. Wolf had dreamed, soon began in Petaluma. On the third Sunday night of the meetings one of the local pastors preached to his congregation against the Seventh-day Adventists. On the fourth Sunday night two other preachers had much to say against the Adventist teachings. After this the opposition continued in one or more of the churches every Sunday night. One preacher said, "If it had simply been the preaching of these men, I would have said nothing against them; but their books are in every house." Whenever possible, a member of the evangelistic group took notes on these talks, and the speakers at the tent reviewed the opposition arguments the following night. Often the opposing ministers were in the audience to listen.

In his extremity one preacher brought some strange views on the subject. He said, "Although the Bible states that the six days of creation week were made up of the evening and the morning, there is no text to tell us that the seventh day, the Sabbath, was that kind of day; it might have been a thousand years in length." Elder Loughborough showed that such a statement made foolishness of God's commandments.

Efforts to Put Out the Fire

How could anyone think that the Creator would ask His people to keep a Sabbath one thousand years long, and command them to refrain from all kinds of work during that thousand years!

Another minister stated that man did not need to keep the Sabbath, for Jesus did away with the Ten Commandment law and replaced it with the *law of love*. The speaker at the tent asked if keeping the law of love meant that we are at liberty to lie and steal and kill and take God's name in vain, breaking nine commandments, as well as the fourth?

It seems almost incredible that any professed ministers of the gospel could have been so ignorant of Biblical and historic facts as were some in those early days.

When the tent meetings began, the Independents took an active part, occupying the front seats, helping with the singing, and agreeing with the speakers' remarks with fervent "Amens." But when the Sabbath question was presented, their leader and several of the other members, including the man who had received the dream, turned against the message and joined those who opposed it. The tent company realized that a knowledge of the truth is not sufficient; there must be a willing heart to obey. In spite of opposition, many remained attentive listeners, and six of the Independents were among the company of twenty organized into a Bible class and Sabbath school when the meetings closed on October 18.

Farmers who brought wheat and other produce from distant ranches to Petaluma often stayed overnight there before making the long trip home. Some of them attended the evening service at the tent. Among them were William Nichols, T. H. Starbuck, and Mr. Dumars, of Windsor, a village twenty-six miles north of Petaluma. The three men approached Elder Bourdeau and said:

"We want you to hold your next course of lectures in Windsor. Some of us are favored in being able to attend these meetings because of business which brings us here, but there are many who cannot come the twenty-six miles. They, too, wish to hear."

After a few days it was arranged that Elder Loughborough should go to Windsor, while Elder Bourdeau would continue the meetings in Petaluma. The rainy season was beginning, and the tent must come down. Evening meetings were held in Petaluma in a rented hall, and Sabbath services and prayer meetings were conducted in a private home. The wives remained to help Elder Bourdeau in his house-to-house visiting, and in organizing a Bible class and Sabbath school.

John Loughborough went alone to break new ground. The village church was offered to him free of charge, and he began meetings on November 4. By the tenth of January, fifty Bible lectures had been given, $50 worth of books had been sold, and a dozen persons had begun keeping the Sabbath. Although the farmers were busy putting in their winter crops of grain, frequently there were as many as two hundred persons in attendance.

Among those who came every night was J. F. Wood. He had come from Walla Walla, Washington, for the definite purpose of getting away from his father-in-law, a Seventh Day Baptist, who was urging him to keep the Sabbath. He had purchased a farm in Windsor and planted grain. As Wood and his family attended the meetings, he began to see that keeping the true Sabbath was really impor-

Efforts to Put Out the Fire

tant. The father-in-law at Walla Walla was overjoyed to receive letters telling of Wood's new-found faith. He and his family read all the literature that was sent them, and wrote Elder Loughborough, asking for a preacher to come to Walla Walla to teach them more of the truth. Elder Loughborough wrote back that he could not leave the work he was starting in California, and that there was no one to send.

The man then wrote to his son-in-law, begging him to come to them; but Wood did not see how he could leave Windsor before he had harvested his grain. As he continued to receive letters urging him to come, he began to think seriously about it. He prayed that if God wanted him to go, He would open the way. Soon after this, a man offered to buy his standing crop of grain. With the money received from this sale, he purchased a lumber wagon with a spring seat, and fitted a canvas over the top. The family and the household goods were loaded into this emigrant wagon, and after a few weeks of travel, they arrived safely at Walla Walla. Here Wood held public meetings, teaching the important truths he had learned in California.

Among the Independents attending the Petaluma tent meetings were two men who were partners in a blacksmith shop. When the lectures started, one of them made the remark, "I love the Lord so sincerely that if He should ask me to lie down on a chopping block and have my head cut off, I would do it in a minute." Mr. Lyttaker, the other man, was quiet and thoughtful. He said little, but he studied much. One day he told his partner that he and his family had decided to keep the Sabbath. The man who had been ready to lay his head on the chopping block answered, "I know the seventh day is the Sabbath, but I cannot keep it. If I did, I could not get work and I would starve to death."

The two men dissolved partnership. Mr. Lyttaker traded his home for a forty-acre farm five miles from Santa Rosa. He built a cabin on his land, by the side of the road, and set up his forge. He had saved an anvil, bellows, and a few tools with which to do blacksmith work on the farm. Every day many wagons with lumber passed his farm on their way to Santa Rosa. Soon the drivers began to leave jobs at his blacksmith shop. In a short time Lyttaker had to enlarge his shop and employ a man to help him. His business soon doubled, and he had a forty-acre farm besides.

Lyttaker begged the ministers to conduct their next course of lectures in his neighborhood. He was sure he could secure the Blakely schoolhouse for their use. On January 31, 1869, Loughborough opened meetings in the settlement called Santa Rosa Creek. In spite of rains and bad roads, he rode horseback from Petaluma to meet the appointment. The audience grew so rapidly that the meetings had to move into a larger schoolhouse in the Piner district. The lectures continued until April 8.

Meanwhile Elder Bourdeau walked four miles and back every other evening to conduct meetings in the Blakely schoolhouse, because a washed-out bridge prevented some of the neighbors from attending at Piner. Thus the winter was a busy one for the two evangelists. Companies of Sabbathkeepers were springing up here and there, and each asked for help. With no heed to weather, the gospel messengers hastened back and forth to meet their appointments, traveling on muddy roads, sometimes on horseback, sometimes with farmers in their wagons.

Efforts to Put Out the Fire 135

At Windsor the second fire had been lighted and was burning brightly. The ministers of the town sounded a warning not to listen to the Adventist preachers or to read their "dangerous literature." They succeeded in turning some away; but oftener their remarks about these "new, strange doctrines" led many to go and hear the lectures. In spite of all the efforts that had been made, flames from that first fire were leaping over county and state border lines, and soon the sparks would cross the ocean to China. One of the new converts at Windsor employed an elderly man named Abram La Rue to chop wood for him. La Rue was a kindly old man with white hair and beard, who had spent most of his life on the sea. He first became interested in the three angels' messages by reading Adventist literature while he was herding sheep. He now attended the meetings and was one of the first converts baptized by Elder Loughborough.

From this time on, Abram La Rue spent time selling or giving away message-filled books and papers. His interest in every person he met and his gentle, persuasive manner led those who received his papers to read them. Hundreds were impressed with the truths they read, and some became missionaries themselves in the homeland and distant countries.

After taking a Bible course at Healdsburg College, La Rue went as a self-supporting missionary to Honolulu, and later to Hong Kong. He paid his way by selling books to captains and sailors on shipboard and around the wharves. His pockets were always filled with papers and tracts, which he handed out freely. He longed for literature which the Chinese people could read. He worked hard, spending only what was needed for the barest necessities of life, and finally he had enough money saved to hire a translator and printer. How happy he was when he had quantities of two small tracts to give to the Chinese people!

The California rains ceased with the coming of spring, and the evangelists pitched their tent on a vacant lot in the Piner district. On April 9, a two-day gathering of all the Sabbathkeepers in the state was opened. In the afternoon, after a baptism, an organization, under the name of "The State Association of Seventh-day Adventists," was formed, to receive tithes and offerings, to build churches, and to arrange for meetings. D. T. Bourdeau was appointed president, John Loughborough, treasurer, and J. F. Wood, secretary.

One of the members, who had kept the first Sabbath after he heard a sermon on that subject at Petaluma, was present. With characteristic promptness he came forward and laid a five-dollar gold piece on the desk, saying, "What is the use of having a treasurer unless you have money in the treasury?"

When the gospel tent was first erected in Petaluma, in 1868, there was only one known Sabbathkeeper in that part of the country. Now there were seventy-five who had signed this covenant:

"We the undersigned hereby associate ourselves together, as a church, taking the name Seventh-day Adventists, covenanting to keep the commandments of God, and the faith of Jesus Christ."

A DAY OF MIRACLES

19

ONE day near the close of the series of meetings in the Piner district, John Loughborough went to Santa Rosa to mail some letters at the post office. As he was walking down the street he was hailed by a doctor and then by one of the merchants, and finally by several leading citizens of the town. "Aren't you going to bring your tent here?" they asked. "The whole town is stirred by that debate you had last week on the Sabbath question. If you want to take advantage of the opening, now is the time to strike." The evangelist had accepted the challenge of an elderly minister who supposed it would be an easy matter to outwit the small, insignificant-looking preacher.

It now seemed that the time had come to accept this invitation and start another fire in the thriving town of Santa Rosa. One of the doctors went with the evangelists to help select a lot on which to erect the tent, and to assist them in finding housekeeping rooms where the ministers' families could live. Merchants supplied lumber for seats and a rostrum. The editor of the county paper offered to print whatever the tent company wanted to write about the coming meetings.

A series of fifty Bible studies began April 22, 1869. One of the studies was on the subject of spiritual gifts, in which it was shown that the gifts of prophecy and of healing, as well as the other special gifts of the Spirit, would be found in the true church to the end of time. The pastor of the largest church in town challenged this statement. He argued that the gifts of the Spirit were given in the days of the apostles for the purpose of establishing the church, and now that the church is established, they are no longer needed. "Healing and other miracles are a thing of the past," he said.

About this time Mrs. Skinner of the Piner district was taken seriously ill, and Dr. Parrot, a graduate from the medical college in Geneva, Switzerland, was called to give advice and treatment. The ministers' wives at the tent asked Dr. Parrot to come to Santa Rosa as soon as her patient was sufficiently recovered, and stay with them for a few days so that she could attend the meetings there.

One day Dr. Parrot decided that her patient was well enough to be left without her for a time. Mrs. Skinner's son Oliver brought a horse, saddled and ready for her to ride to Santa Rosa, and another horse for himself. He was to go with her and bring back the horse she was riding. For some reason the horse, when the woman mounted it, began to rear and pitch. She fell to the ground, and the horse fell on top of her in such a way that the saddle struck across her arms and chest with such force that it bent the saddle horn. When her friends picked her up and carried her into the house, they feared that she was dead.

After a time she regained consciousness and began to speak in a whisper. Someone suggested, "We'd better send for a doctor."

A Day of Miracles

"No!" she gasped. "A doctor can do me no good. Send for the ministers at the tent. If they come and pray for me, the Lord will heal me."

Early in the morning the ministers and their wives arrived in a lumber wagon. They found the doctor suffering such pain that when she was moved she fainted. In a whisper, she said, "Anoint me and pray, and the Lord will heal me." Mrs. Loughborough anointed her, and the ministers prayed that the Great Physician would do for her what no earthly doctor could do.

Almost immediately the pain left her body, and she began to pray in a clear, strong voice. Her face lighted up with joy. She clapped her hands together and in a strong voice said, "I am healed." She arose, dressed herself, and went into another bedroom, where Mrs. Skinner was recovering. Then the doctor helped prepare dinner for her guests. That afternoon she rode to Santa Rosa in a chair placed in the lumber wagon, and she attended the evening service.

Oliver Skinner considered himself to be an infidel. But when he saw how God had answered prayer, he told everyone about it. He had to repeat the story again and again to those who came to find out if it was really true.

The next Sunday the minister who had preached against spiritual gifts asserted more positively than before that the day of miracles was past. He made light of the report of Dr. Parrot's healing, saying that her suffering could have been easily feigned for effect. These remarks advertised the matter; and some who had never heard of it before went to see Oliver and to inquire if what had been told them was actually true. They knew that the young man had always professed to be an infidel, and they expected him to join those who were ridiculing the matter.

He said, "Gentlemen, I know what I am talking about. I was one of the attendants who worked all night after the accident to keep the doctor alive. The facts are those men and women prayed, and Dr. Parrot got up entirely relieved of all pain. I sat on the porch and heard them pray. I saw the doctor come out of the bedroom fully dressed. I saw her walk into my mother's room. I ate of the dinner that she helped to prepare; and I went with her in the wagon that brought her to Santa Rosa." After hearing the young man's report, many went away saying, "It must be that God is still working miracles for His people, as He did in the days of the apostles."

A young woman whom the community knew had been a bedfast invalid for several months was unable to get out of bed to attend the meetings. She was so much interested in what her family told her of the Bible studies that she persuaded one of the ministers to visit her and give a synopsis of each sermon.

One day she heard that several converts were to be baptized in Santa Rosa Creek. She said, "I, too, want to be baptized."

Her husband asked, "How can you be?"

She answered, "The Lord has heard my prayers and forgiven my sins, and He will give me strength to be baptized."

On the day of the baptism the young wife was dressed for the occasion and placed in a chair. The chair was then lifted and set in a wagon, and the team was driven into shallow water. Two men lifted the chair from the wagon, and Elder Loughborough took hold of the chair on one side and Elder

A Day of Miracles   141

Bourdeau on the other and they carried her to a place where the water was deeper, and baptized her. As they lifted her out of the water, she shouted, "Glory." Her face was shining with the joy of the Lord. She walked to the wagon without assistance, got into it without help, changed her clothing at the house, and prepared dinner for the company, declaring that she was a well woman.

How surprised the people were the following Sabbath to see her climb out of the wagon, walk into the tent, sit through the services on a hard board bench, then ride three miles to her brother-in-law's home, and return for the evening meeting! At its close she rode again in the uncomfortable lumber wagon. From the day of her baptism she was able to do her own housework and was not known to spend another day in bed until near the time of her death. The townsfolk who knew of her long illness were ready to agree with the Adventist ministers, who said that the day of miracles had not passed.

The Santa Rosa meetings closed with forty persons signing the covenant. The tent was next moved to Healdsburg, where Elder Bourdeau opened a series of Bible lectures. For his subject the first evening he took the motto that waved above the tent, "What Is Truth?"

Mr. Ferguson made arrangements for Elder Loughborough to hold a meeting the next Sunday at the Monroe schoolhouse, three miles from Santa Rosa. Early the previous Sabbath morning the minister was given a saddle horse to ride to his appointment at the Monroe schoolhouse. A mile from the schoolhouse he passed a man hauling a load of wood. "Elder," he said, "you're going to have trouble today. Old Morton says he'll not let you into the schoolhouse." When Elder Loughborough arrived at the place, he tied his horse back of the building, and with Bible and hymnbook in hand, walked into the schoolhouse. Several of the sisters were already inside, but the men were out in front, and Morton was talking to them in such an excited manner that he did not see the minister enter the building. He was saying, "Loughborough shall not go into that house today."

"He's in there right now," one of the men said.

Hearing this, Mr. Morton rushed into the schoolroom, shouting, "Get out of this house, you liar, you thief and blasphemer." He seized Elder Loughborough's arm with a fierce grasp, pulled him out the door and into the road, saying as he did so, "You stole my son. You're a blasphemer, saying the soul is not immortal."

Elder Loughborough attempted to answer these charges and to explain that the son had himself determined to be baptized. Morton did not give the minister a chance to speak. The angry man began to swing a cane over his head, as though he were going to strike him. Some of the onlookers became alarmed. One brawny fellow pulled off his coat, saying, "Elder, let me pitch into that man. He shan't abuse you so."

The little minister calmly answered, "Just keep your coat on, brother, and let him alone. He is really helping more than hurting us."

Then another man stepped up to Morton and said, "It's a good thing this didn't happen a few weeks ago. I profess to be a Christian now and don't believe it's right for a Christian to be angry. Six weeks ago I'd have laid you on your back for talking this way to the elder."

Morton, a trustee of the schoolhouse, refused to allow the meeting to be held there. "Well, it is a fine day," the elder said cheerfully. "When the rest get here, we'll have our meeting under the shade of some of these live oaks." Then turning to the man who had threatened him, Loughborough said, "I've no ill will toward you, Mr. Morton. I wish you well. Someday you'll learn you're mistaken in your opposition."

At the close of the outdoor service a Mr. Hewitt called the minister aside and said, "Brother Loughborough, we must have a meetinghouse of our own."

He replied, "Well, this is the Sabbath. We won't build meetinghouses today."

"We must have a meetinghouse of our own," persisted Hewitt. "I'll give the church a deed to the two lots on which the tent was pitched in Santa Rosa and $500 in cash besides."

Later another brother, Mr. Walker, a contractor, called Mr. Loughborough aside and made a similar suggestion: "The way things are shaping, we'll have to have a meetinghouse of our own. I'll superintend the job of erecting it and give $100 in cash besides."

The people were of one mind, and soon there were pledges for $1,340, besides many offers of free labor.

That evening John Loughborough went to Healdsburg to hear Elder Bourdeau's sermon on the subject of Daniel 7. The next Friday evening, after preaching at the tent, the Loughboroughs, with their son Delmer, rode with the Nichols family to stay overnight. Early Sabbath morning, before breakfast, they drove on to Mrs. Skinner's in the Piner district, where the Sabbath services were to be held.

While they were eating breakfast, Mrs. Skinner told them that a Mr. Peugh had been persuaded to believe that the ministers were Mormons. He had nailed fast the windows and doors of the schoolhouse and announced to his friends that Loughborough shall not enter that house again. He sharpened a huge butcher knife, prepared a long club, and boasted that he was going to waylay the preacher as he came into the neighborhood.

Glancing out the window after breakfast at the Skinners, the minister saw Peugh going down the road! It was the only road from Healdsburg the Loughboroughs could come, and the angry man was going to meet him.

The elder smiled, "Hope he'll have a good time up the road waiting for me."

When Oliver Skinner and the Loughboroughs reached the schoolhouse, the former unlocked the door. He had not told anyone that he was armed with a loaded revolver. The Sabbath school and services were conducted without any disturbance. A little time before the closing hymn, Mr. Peugh came into the yard much bewildered, wondering how the minister had managed to pass without his seeing him. At the close of the meeting, the brethren formed a circle around the angry man, as Elder Loughborough, with his wife and Delmer, passed out of the building to their carriage and drove away.

This experience urged the Sabbathkeepers forward in their plea, "We must have a meetinghouse of our own." They backed up their plea with more pledges to the church-building fund. Not long after this, Mr. Peugh acknowledged his mistake and was heard to remark, "If anybody has good religion, it's the kind Loughborough has."

A Day of Miracles

On October 11, 1869, while in the midst of a series of tent meetings in Sebastopol, Elder and Mrs. Loughborough drove over to Santa Rosa to see the foundation of the new church building laid. When they arrived they found the foundation already laid, and the members had made it ten feet longer than the brethren had voted. "We added ten feet, agreeing among ourselves we would meet the expense of the extra length," said the builders.

"California style of liberality," was John Loughborough's reply as he surveyed their work.

About the last of November the rains began, and the tent was stored for the winter. The evangelists moved into one of Mr. Hewitt's houses near the new church. They were nicely settled in time for the Bourdeaus to welcome a baby daughter, whom they named Patience.

THE PROSPECTOR

∽20∾

ONE morning as John Loughborough was studying in the empty meeting tent, the mail stage drove up. "Here, elder, is a letter for you," called out the driver. The letter was from Gold Hill, Nevada, and was addressed "To the Elders at the Tent at Healdsburg, California." It told how a prospector, William Hunt, had returned to his camp after a weary day working with pick and shovel. He sat down in his cabin to read his weekly paper, the *California Christian Advocate*. As he read he came to an editorial telling about two ministers who were holding meetings in a big tent. The writer of the article advised the public to stay away from the fanatical Adventists. He ridiculed them, calling them Millerites. This editorial was not of any special interest to the old man, but reading helped him forget his aching back and limbs.

He read on, "The men conducting the meetings neither preach nor pray, but simply harangue the gaping crowds on prophecy. They have books to sell on Daniel and the Revelation." Suddenly he came to life. "What's that!" he exclaimed. "Books on Daniel and the Revelation! That's just what I want." He sat down at once and wrote a letter, asking for the book on the Revelation.

In his letter he said, "Now for twenty years I have been studying that book, and I have written to New York, Philadelphia, and other places to get some treatise explaining it, but have failed. I wish you would forward to me by Wells Fargo Express one of the books that you are selling on Revelation. Send it C.O.D., and I will remit the pay, and be greatly obliged to you."

Upon receipt of the letter, Elder Loughborough made up a package containing the book on the Revelation, all the tracts that had been printed up to that time relating to any of the prophecies on Daniel, one on the Saviour's prophecy in Matthew 24, one on spiritism, and a few others. These he sent to Hunt by post. He wrote a letter to go with the package, telling him about the *Review and Herald* weekly, and giving the names of other books he might want to obtain. "You may send me a $2.50 gold piece in a Wells Fargo envelope, to square the account," he wrote. On learning what Elder Loughborough had done, an old Californian asked, "Why didn't you send the books by Wells Fargo, C.O.D., as Hunt suggested? You're running quite a risk; I'm afraid you'll never hear from that man again."

"Because it is cheaper to send the books by post," replied the economical preacher. "Besides, if I do not hear from him, the books will do him or somebody else some good anyway."

About two weeks after this he received another letter from Gold Hill, and a notice from Wells Fargo, asking him to call and sign for a money envelope at the post office. The letter said, "Please excuse my delay in writing you. When I received that package of books from you I could take no time for writing until I had read through the entire lot. I am now reading them a second time. I hope you will keep on writing me, for I do not want to lose track of your whereabouts. I want the *Review and Herald* sent me for a year, and the other books you mentioned in your letter. I send you by Wells Fargo $20. Take out the pay for the paper and books, and put the rest in your pocket for yourself."

Elder Loughborough forwarded Mr. Hunt's *Review and Herald* subscription to the office. He sent him another package of books and tracts, and told him that he would not keep the balance of the money himself, but would put it to his credit to pay for other books that he might wish to order later.

In answer to this, there came another letter from Mr. Hunt, expressing thanks for the books, and containing notice of another $20 at Wells Fargo, which he was sending to help with the expenses of the meetings. Then Elder Loughborough did an unusual thing. He wrote back, telling Hunt that he must not think it his duty to sustain the meetings. He must not cramp himself by sending money that he needed.

In answer to this, there came another $20 from Hunt, and a letter in which he said: "I think I had better get some of my money where it will do some good. I have received great light from the publications you have sent, and I accept the whole truth as taught in them. I am shaping my affairs so that I can keep the seventh-day Sabbath." In this manner the correspondence continued, until Hunt had a copy of everything published by the denomination. He also asked the ministers to be sure and send their new postal address when they moved.

The Adventist workers said, "Surely we need never be alarmed by the reproaches that the enemies of truth hurl against us. That editorial in the *Advocate* has done more good than harm. It has brought the knowledge of these precious books to a man who was seeking for truth."

About a year after this, in May, 1870, while holding meetings in Bloomfield, Elder Loughborough noticed in the audience a man who gave good attention to every word spoken. At the close of the lecture one of the members brought the visitor forward, and introduced him, saying, "Here's a man from Nevada who wants to talk to you. He's stopping at our lodging house."

"And is his name William Hunt," asked the minister, "with whom I have been corresponding for more than a year?"

"Yes, I'm the man," said the stranger. "I've come to spend a few days before leaving the States. I'm on my way to New Zealand—or perhaps the diamond fields of South Africa." He remained a few days to attend the meetings, and then was off, taking with him a set of the charts and all the literature that could be spared. Hunt's parting message was, "I'll probably never see you again; but you'll hear from me if I get through safely. By the Lord's help I shall faithfully obey the truth."

About three years later Elder Loughborough received a letter from Hunt. Living at the diamond fields in Africa, he was faithfully distributing literature among the mine workers. He was making his living by washing tailings from the mines, in search of chip diamonds, which at the time were in great demand.

There was an interesting sequence to this experience, which was not known until some years afterward. A young man named Petrus Wessels was living on a farm not far from the mines. He contracted tuberculosis and failed so rapidly that in a short time all hope of his recovery was gone. A sympathetic friend handed him a tract on divine healing. After reading the tract he went to his minister and asked that special prayer be offered for his healing. But the minister refused, fearing that he might be thought fanatical if he did such an unusual thing.

Wessels was in earnest about the matter. He knelt at his bedside and told the Lord that he had done his best to get someone to pray for him, but he had failed. He then and there made a vow to the Lord that if He would heal him, he would obey whatever instructions he should find in the Bible. Soon he was a well man!

He and his brothers were in the dairy business, which required much Sunday work. This troubled Peter, for he felt he was not keeping his vow. He suggested to his older brother that they dispose of the dairy and take up some other occupation that would give them an opportunity to keep the Sabbath day holy.

His brother replied, "If you are going to be so particular about Sabbathkeeping, why don't you keep the right day? The commandment says to keep the seventh day." He pointed to the calendar and showed Peter that Sunday was the first day of the week, not the seventh; when, to his astonishment, his conscientious brother answered, "If the Bible says to keep the seventh day, I'll keep it."

Peter Wessels went to pray. Then, not knowing much about the Bible, he opened it at random, and his eye fell on the words, "In the end of the Sabbath, as it began to dawn toward the first day of the week." He read the verse aloud and said to himself, "Then the Sabbath is not the first day of the week; it is not Sunday. I must keep the seventh day, the day which God commands us to keep holy, for I have promised to obey the Bible in everything. But how can I keep Saturday, when everybody else is keeping Sunday?"

In his perplexity he went to talk the matter over with his friend, Van Druten. The friend answered, "There's an old miner around here who keeps Saturday for Sunday. I've been reading some of his tracts, and I believe he is right." Together they went to see the old man—William Hunt! After a few evenings spent in study, Hunt convinced both men that he had the truth, not only about the Sabbath, but about many other Bible doctrines. They joined Hunt in distributing the Sabbath tracts and in passing the truth along to everyone who would listen.

Finally Mr. Van Druten wrote a letter to the General Conference in Battle Creek, asking for a missionary to come and teach them more fully. With the letter he sent £50, worth $250 at that time, to pay the traveling expenses of the missionary. Within a year not only one missionary, but several, were sent them. The group included Elders C. L. Boyd and D. A. Robinson, with their families and several colporteurs. A few years later fifteen young people were on their way from South Africa to Battle Creek to attend college and prepare for gospel service in their homeland.

THE FIRST CAMP MEETING IN CALIFORNIA

21

IN OCTOBER, 1872, Elder Loughborough was more than busy helping the brethren at Windsor get ready to hold the first camp meeting in California. A letter was received from Elder James White in response to a long-standing invitation for him and his wife to come to California. He said that they were planning to reach the West Coast by the first of October, and they would be happy to meet with the new believers in a general camp meeting. That meant quick action to notify the churches in Woodland and San Francisco, as well as the five companies in the Sonoma Valley, for there were no telephones in those days.

In 1870, Elder Bourdeau had been called to labor again in the East, and Elder Cornell had taken his place in California. This autumn Elder Cornell was conducting a tent effort at Woodland, so it fell to Elder Loughborough to hurry from place to place, announcing the camp meeting and advising the church members what to bring with them—food, bedding, camping outfits, material for building shelters, ticks to fill with straw for mattresses, and whatever else they might need for a week's camping.

The First Camp Meeting in California

Elder Loughborough described the appearance of the campground in these words:

"In the hasty preparation for the meeting our tents were a variety indeed. Some few were regular camping tents, some were rough board shanties, some were sheets fastened onto wooden frames, some of the brethren and sisters in their haste took up their rag carpets and put them over frames of wood. In the case of one brother who did not hear of the meeting until the night before it was to commence, he came to the camp, and we made him a tent by piling in fence rails between stakes driven close together, covering it with rails, and a shawl served as a door to the tent. The weather was fair and dry; so no one suffered, and all were rejoicing to be gathered in camp."

After three days of hard work, temporary abodes were ready for thirty-three families. The evangelistic effort in Woodland was closed for a short time, and the gospel tent brought to Windsor to serve as the main auditorium. At the end of the third day the weary workers looked the camp over and announced with satisfaction that all was in readiness for the meetings to begin. October 2 the camp meeting was opened with a sermon by Elder White.

During the six days of meeting, Elder and Mrs. White spoke thirteen times. Monday there was a baptism, and on Tuesday, the closing day, Merritt G. Kellogg was ordained to the gospel ministry. The tent was then taken down and moved back to Woodland, and the evangelistic effort was resumed. By this time winter was approaching, and it was necessary to set up a big stove in the tent to drive out the evening chill.

In the previous May the tent had been pitched in a vacant

lot in Woodland across from the courthouse. From the first night's service there had been a good interest among the town's leading citizens. In attendance were the deputy sheriff, the county treasurer, the cashier of the bank, the court crier, and John Kelly, an ex-member of the state legislature.

The Woodland *Weekly News* gave this report of the meetings: "Passing up the main street, stop where you will. All you hear is concerning the teachers in the tent. There has been an awakening of dry bones; a shaking of dust from the backs of old and neglected Bibles; a refreshing of memory in regard to ourselves and what that Book proposes to do for us—a subject which has become rusty since the days of mother and home; a general inquiry in regard to matters, which follow the first question—'Have you been to the tent?' Some are serious, some thoughtful, some inclined to sneer. One thing is certain, the excitement is general. The tent has been crowded nightly, and everybody seems to be dissatisfied with home when the vesper stars appear."

On the second Sunday, when nearly a thousand persons were in attendance, the court crier arose and said, "These men are talking to us about things in which we are deeply interested. They have made no call for help, but we want to do something to help them along with these interesting meetings. I am going to take up a collection, and I want all of you to go down into your pockets and hand out freely." He passed his white beaver hat, and gold and silver coins were dropped in to the amount of $51.55.

Again on the following Sunday night he stood up and said, "I am not satisfied with the collection which we took last Sunday evening; we did not get enough. There are others here, too, that want to show their appreciation of what these men are doing. And now, although the ministers shake their heads, I am going to take another collection; so go down into your pockets and hand out liberally." Around went the beaver hat again, and the coins clinked as they fell in. The total for the two evenings was $92.65.

When the Windsor camp meeting closed and the ministers were back in Woodland, they naturally felt that they were among old friends. At the close of the series a church was organized. While the evangelists were busy planning for a meetinghouse and raising the necessary funds, John Kelly was secretly collecting a purse for them. One evening, to their surprise, he handed them $100 in gold coin. The man was truly surprised when they refused to accept it for themselves, and insisted on handing it over to the treasurer of the building fund. This act pleased the people in general, and after that they gave even more liberally.

Early in the winter of 1873, Elder Loughborough held a series of Bible lectures in the vicinity of Red Bluff. In that neighborhood there lived a woman who had made the remark, "I shall not go to hear that man; I would just as soon hear a dog bark as to hear him preach." About the time the meetings opened, one of her daughters was taken violently ill with a fever. As soon as the elder heard of it, he called on the family and showed the mother how to give the patient a wet-sheet pack. The treatment brought immediate relief, and after a second treatment the girl was well. After that the entire family attended the meetings, and all accepted the message. One daughter later became a Bible instructor.

Elder Loughborough obtained permission to hold meetings in the Red Bluff courthouse. A man named Wilkins was employed as bookkeeper for one of the business firms in town. He was suffering with tuberculosis, though still able to carry on his work. A few weeks before this the mother had met Mrs. White on the train coming from Philadelphia. They talked together regarding the ailing son, and Mrs. White gave the mother advice about his care. She also gave her some copies of the health journal. Later, when the son saw the notice of the meetings in the courthouse, he said, "Mother, I wonder if that man is not one of Mrs. White's people. I am going to his meeting to see, and if he is, I am going to ask him home with me." They both attended the meetings regularly; and within a month the mother and son were baptized.

In May, 1873, the tent was pitched at Napa and later in Saint Helena, and churches were organized in both places.

The Napa *Register* described the meetings in these words: "The Adventists, who have been here holding their tent meetings, are now attracting the general attention and causing 'the dry bones to shake.' Elder Cornell is nightly drawing large, attentive, orderly, and appreciative audiences, and is winning golden opinions both for his gentlemanly bearing and the masterly and intelligent manner in which he elucidates the subjects presented. One 'hot gospeler' had the temerity to attack the elder recently, and failing to draw him into rough, browbeating, undignified style of discussion, straightened the laps of his coat to the zephyrs and no longer intruded his presence upon an order-loving, dignified assemblage of Saint Helena's proverbially quiet and polite inhabitants. The peculiar tenets of these people may be wrong; but the advocates are entitled to respect no less for their self-sacrificing zeal and earnestness and their genial, gentlemanly deportment."

In September a nine-day camp meeting was held in Yountville, in the Napa Valley about midway between the two towns. There were fifty-three family tents on the grounds, and twenty-nine persons were baptized. At one of the meetings a man named Moses G. Church, who had been visiting relatives in Napa County, arose and said, "I am engaged in constructing an irrigation canal from Kings River. I have forty men in my employ, but from this time that work shall all stop on the Lord's Sabbath." At his invitation, gospel work was commenced at Fresno, his home town, and farther south.

The Disciples Church had a large congregation at Yountville. The year before at Woodland, Pastor Martin, a professor of the Disciple College, had held a debate with Elder Cornell. Not satisfied with the results, and thinking to gain the confidence of his members at Yountville, he challenged Elder Cornell to a second debate. The time assigned was during the last two days of the camp meeting.

At the close of the debate a member of Professor Martin's congregation asked that a collection be taken to pay his expenses to and from the place. As soon as this suggestion was made, another man arose in the audience and suggested that the collection be divided between the two debaters. Finally it was decided to place two hats on the table, one for Mr. Martin and one for Mr. Cornell. As the audience passed out, each person was asked to put his offering into the hat of the one whom he considered the victor in the debate. When the money was counted, it was found that the professor's hat had only $2.50 in it, while Cornell's had about $30.

BEGINNINGS IN OAKLAND

22

JOHN LOUGHBOROUGH was glad to be associated again with his friends, Elder and Mrs. James White, and to have their assistance. Elder Loughborough had many questions to ask regarding the progress of the work in the East, for he had received only the brief reports he had read in the *Review and Herald*.

A year after the Loughboroughs left on their mission to California, James Erzberger had arrived in Battle Creek from Switzerland, with a copy of the *Review* in his hand to identify himself. He was looking for the people who would instruct him more fully in the three angels' messages. For some time after his arrival he had been a guest in the White family, and had spent every moment of his time acquiring a knowledge of the English language. Edson and Willie White and John Kellogg took turns walking around with him, pointing out various objects, naming them, and talking about them. They were young lads, and at the time, were attending classes conducted by Professor G. H. Bell in the frame building that had first housed the *Review and Herald* publishing house. Soon Erzberger was able to join in conversation with the family; and in a few weeks he was ready to go with the Whites to the camp meetings and to give talks in his newly acquired tongue.

Professor Bell's classes had developed into a school, sponsored by the General Conference, which later was to develop into the Battle Creek College. His work was based on sound educational principles and the instruction received through the Bible and the spirit of prophecy. He also put heart and soul into the building up of Sabbath schools. He had written two splendid series of Sabbath-school lessons for *The Youth's Instructor,* which was now being printed semimonthly. His aim was to train the youth in the habit of deep, thorough study of the Sabbath-school lessons, as well as of their day-school lessons.

Doubtless Elders Loughborough and White expressed their joy over the rapid expansion of the tent-meeting and camp-meeting programs, which were conducted in nearly all the state conferences.

John reviewed the wonderful providences connected with the work in California, and he answered questions regarding the welfare of his own family. Recently he and Maggie had gone through a sorrowful experience in the death of their five-month-old baby girl, Elizabeth Eunice. We can hear Ellen repeating to the bereaved mother the precious promises of God's word which had been a comfort to her, for Mrs. White had suffered likewise in the death of her own little John Herbert.

Some of us have tried to appreciate the difficulties of those pioneer wives; but the full realization of their sufferings will be impossible in these days of comfortable homes, modern household appliances, and scientifically prepared baby foods, baby clinics, pediatricians, and visiting nurses.

When one considers the financial straits in which the messengers of truth were often placed, which made the obtaining of suitable and nourishing food for the mother almost impossible, it is not hard to understand why there were so many little graves in those days.

Mrs. J. O. Corliss once told of a winter she spent with two of her children in a shanty during her husband's absence from home. The snow blew in through cracks in the wooden floor and walls. She wrapped the children's feet and legs in rags, because she had no money with which to buy stockings and shoes. Did she write a complaining letter to her husband, begging him to come home and get a job and support his family? No! That was not the spirit of those brave pioneer mothers.

In December, 1872, the Whites made their home for the winter in the Loughborough house in Santa Rosa, and they spent much time itinerating among the new churches in the Sonoma Valley. At Bloomfield the California Conference was organized on February 15 and 16, 1873, with two hundred thirty-eight Sabbathkeepers in the state. Elder Loughborough was elected president, a position he retained until 1878. Soon the Whites were on their way east to attend a session of the General Conference that was to be held in March; but by the end of the year they were back again in California, preaching, counseling, planning for the upbuilding of various branches of the work.

While visiting among the churches, Elder White looked about for a suitable place to establish the publishing house and start printing a paper. One day in April, 1874, while he and his wife were crossing San Francisco Bay, they remarked upon the dense crowds of people on the ferry. When they reached Oakland, Mrs. White said, "James, this is the place I told you about, that I saw in a vision. I did not know the name of the city; but there was a large body of water, and hundreds of people were crossing and recrossing every day. Somewhere in Oakland is the place to publish the paper."

At once Elder White made definite plans to locate the publishing house in Oakland and to start printing a paper to be called the *Signs of the Times*. He and his wife moved from Santa Rosa and rented rooms on the outskirts of Oakland. They felt that the time had come to build up a strong church in that city. Early in the spring the tent was erected in a central place, and a series of meetings begun by Elders D. M. Canright and M. E. Cornell.

Soon after the meetings opened, a temperance "local option" movement was launched in the city. As there was no hall large enough to accommodate the crowds, the Adventist ministers offered the temperance forces the use of their tent, and joined in a great temperance rally. For ten days the question of liquor or no liquor held the attention of the city, with the final victory on the side of temperance. The church bells rang, and there was great rejoicing. This kindly act won for the Adventist preachers the sympathies of the best citizens in town; and when the attention of the people was again turned to the study of the prophetic word, the tent was well filled with attentive and interested listeners.

During this time a second new tent was pitched in East Oakland, and a similar invitation was given the temperance societies in that section. In appreciation for a few days' use of these two tents, the temperance forces made appropriations amounting to $250 to the evangelistic efforts.

James White, in his search for a suitable place in the city in which to print the paper, found a small printing outfit for sale at a reasonable price. In order to prove the type, he had the first issues of the *Signs* set up there. The first issue was dated June 4, 1874. Before the printed pages were folded and taken to the post office, they were spread out on the floor, as Elder and Mrs. White, with their son Edson and his wife, and Elder Loughborough, bowed in earnest prayer. The printing outfit was purchased, the room it occupied was rented, and six numbers of the *Signs* were printed before Elder White went east to attend the camp meetings and the General Conference held in Battle Creek in August, 1874, where he presented to the brethren the need of establishing a publishing house in the West.

By July, Elder Loughborough had helped the Oakland evangelistic companies organize a church of about fifty members. Another room was rented in the same building adjoining the type room, but larger, and was fitted out for a meeting hall with lamps, carpet, and one hundred chairs.

From October 2 to 11 a second camp meeting was held at Yountville. This was the third camp meeting in California. The two sixty-foot gospel tents were pitched side by side, with a piece of canvas spliced between, forming a large assembly tent, sixty by one hundred twenty feet. There were eighty-five family tents and more than five hundred campers on the grounds.

Mrs. Loughborough had contracted tuberculosis from a patient she had nursed for a short time in her home. In order that her husband's public labors should not be interrupted, her sister had come from the East to care for her. While seeking a more favorable place for the patient, they had made their home first in Woodland and then in Saint Helena. As Mrs. Loughborough was too weak to attend the Yountville meetings, a tent was pitched for her and her sister back of the assembly tent, near to the rostrum, where she could lie on her bed and listen to the services, and especially the reports, in which she was greatly interested.

It had been six years since the two evangelists, Loughborough and Bourdeau, had opened the first series of tent meetings in Petaluma. The California days of pioneering had seen the work grow into a conference of fourteen churches, able to support itself and to send workers on to new fields. These California churches had returned to the General Conference more than the amount of money expended in sending the first two missionaries and their equipment, and in supporting them until the work there was self-sustaining.

Elder and Mrs. White were in the East at the time of this camp meeting. Before leaving, Elder White had promised to endeavor to raise $6,000 in the East for the establishment of the publishing work on the Pacific Coast, if the California brethren would meet it with $4,000. Elder G. I. Butler presented this proposition to those gathered at the camp meeting. He offered, however, the alternative of requesting the *Review and Herald* to open a book depository on the coast. The members resolved enthusiastically to have a publishing house of their own, and immediately, without any urging, pledges were made totaling $19,414, and by January 1, 1876, when the pledges were due, $20,000 had been paid into the fund.

In the afternoon of the same day, Elder Loughborough told the people that he had intended to call for a tent and camp-meeting fund of $500; but as they had pledged so liberally in the morning, he did not feel free at that time to ask them for more. "Try us on it," said T. M. Chapman, "and see if we will not raise a tent and camp-meeting fund. I'm willing to start this fund off with a pledge of $50." In a few minutes, pledges to the tent fund climbed to $1,616.20. When the time came for the payments to be closed, $1,700 had been turned in.

No wonder Elder Butler wrote, "We have financial strength in this state sufficient to do almost anything we wish to undertake. There is a stability to this cause here; it is of no mushroom growth. When responsible persons come forward and pledge over $21,000 of yellow gold to sustain and forward the work going on in its midst, all will agree that it means business. It is no wonder that ministers and members of our staid, respectable popular churches are astonished at such a result."

As Maggie Loughborough lay on her bed, praying and listening to all that was said in the assembly tent, her heart thrilled at these indications of the glorious forward march of the message she loved so dearly. She rejoiced in the blessed hope and was fully resigned to her death, which came in the spring of 1875.

CLOSING YEARS

23

AS THE work grew stronger in California, Elder Loughborough was called for ministerial service farther away. He had become acquainted with Anna M. Driscol, the secretary and treasurer of the Pacific Press Publishing Association, where Elder Loughborough was president of the publishing house. The couple were married by Elder James White.

In 1877 the pioneering leader took a coastal steamer from San Francisco to Portland, Oregon, where he was met by his friend, Elder I. D. Van Horn. Together they conducted meetings Sabbath and Sunday, and then started for Walla Walla. At five o'clock in the morning they boarded a small freighter that chugged up the Columbia River. In a few hours they came to the Cascades. Here all the freight had to be unloaded and carried on men's shoulders to a train, which carried it three miles to another river boat. By four o'clock in the afternoon all cargo was on the second boat, and the next seven hours were spent steaming up the river. Again they transferred to a train and back to another steamer, where, after waiting all night, the trip was resumed Tuesday morning. Before sundown they reached another stopping place. Here the passengers got off the boat and took rooms for the night. Wednesday morning at nine o'clock they boarded the train again, reaching Walla Walla about noon, fifty-five hours after leaving Portland. It is hard to realize that three quarters of a century later this short trip can be made by airplane in about an hour!

In midsummer, 1878, Elder Loughborough, accompanied by Mrs. White and a lady friend, took passage on the steamer "Oregon" to attend the first camp meeting in the Pacific Northwest. He brought with him a new tent and a number of family tents which were loaned from the California Conference. The camp was pitched in a pine grove near the State Fair Grounds at Salem. The Maxons and Woods, who ten years before had pioneered the work in that north country, were among the campers. Mrs. Wood led out in the singing, and she also played the organ. William Nichols gave his time freely to the task of managing the dining tent in order that a profit might be realized to apply on the camp-meeting expenses. Everyone, from the oldest to the youngest, helped make the occasion a grand success. On the last Sunday, Mrs. White spoke to a large audience from the music stand in the city park, and again on Tuesday evening at the Methodist church.

In the spring of 1878, Elder Loughborough answered a call from a group of California believers who had moved to the State of Nevada. They wrote requesting that a minister be sent to open up work at Saint Clair. His labors there for a period of only a few weeks resulted in doubling the membership of ten in the company, and the raising of sufficient money to pay his traveling expenses to Nevada and to purchase a fifty-foot tent for use in the state.

Closing Years

On September 19, 1878, Elder Loughborough and his wife boarded a tourist Pullman en route to Battle Creek. From there, after a few days' pause, they proceeded to England. Nearly eleven years had passed since the two pioneering ministers, Loughborough and Bourdeau, had made the month-long voyage with their families, by the way of Panama, from New York to San Francisco. These had been years of tireless and fruitful toil. The newly established churches were growing rapidly, and new companies were springing up. Efficient workers had been sent from the East to California or had been trained through local evangelistic efforts. It was felt that Elder Loughborough should add his experience to the efforts that were being made to introduce the message into England.

John Loughborough preached his first sermon at Shirley Hall, Southampton. About the middle of May a sixty-foot tent was erected in the city, and seventy-four lectures were given. The attendance was good, but the response much slower than in America. It was not until February 8, 1880, that the first baptism was held in Great Britain, at which time there were six candidates. By July, 1881, twenty-nine had been brought into the faith. Elder Loughborough returned to America to attend the twentieth session of the General Conference, which convened December 1, 1881. His son Delmer and a daughter accompanied him when he returned to England, to assist him in his work. After six years of labor, the elder returned to his homeland to spend the remaining forty years of his life helping to instruct and strengthen the Adventist believers, collecting funds and starting new enterprises, traveling from church to church and from camp meeting to camp meeting, telling the story of what he had witnessed of God's wonderful providences.

Early in the twentieth century Elder Loughborough moved to Mountain View, where he built a neat cottage, planted trees and flowers, and looked forward to years of happiness with his wife. The dream was soon marred, however, for Anna died on May 31, 1907.

In the days that I best remember him, his favorite themes were signs in the heavens of Christ's soon coming and God's leadership of this denomination through the gift of prophecy. He had seen Mrs. White in vision more than forty times. He had stood shoulder to shoulder with Elder White when they raised the necessary funds and pioneered in the establishment of the Pacific Press Publishing Association, the Saint Helena Sanitarium, and other institutions on the Pacific Coast. In his lifetime he watched the advent movement grow from a few scattered companies of disappointed and disheartened believers to a strong, well-organized body, with general, union, and state conferences, with churches, schools, publishing houses, sanitariums, and missions, extending throughout the world.

During his long span of years he saw the invention of the telegraph, the telephone, electric lights, moving pictures, the automobile, radio, and the airplane. At the age of seventy-seven he made a sixteen-month trip around the world, visiting churches, mission schools, and other institutions. During this time he traveled 30,000 miles by sea and 17,500 miles on land. He attended 500 meetings and preached 352 times. In speaking of this trip, he said, "During my voyage over eleven seas, I was never sick a day or missed a meal. I tripped the deck each day and felt like a boy."

After his return he had a physical checkup and received

from the physician the report of a sound body, normal temperature, pulse, and blood pressure. His last seven years were spent at the Saint Helena Sanitarium, where we had the privilege of frequent visits with him, sometimes in my father's home, and at other times on the lawn under the great oaks in front of the sanitarium building. Shortly before his death he stated he had read the Bible through more than seventy times! During the greater part of his busy life, he read systematically all Adventist periodicals issued from the denominational publishing houses. As each magazine came in the mail, he would open it, lay it on a pile with others, and then, as he had time, he would begin at the top of the pile and read every word to the last page.

On April 7, 1924, at the age of ninety-two, he quietly fell asleep, and was laid to rest in the Saint Helena cemetery, where many of his fellow laborers are now resting. They await the call of the Life-giver to glory and immortality. "They that be wise shall shine as the brightness of the firmament; and they that turn many to righteousness as the stars for ever and ever."

We'd love to have you download our catalog of titles we publish at:

www.TEACHServices.com

or write or email us your thoughts, reactions, or criticism about this or any other book we publish at:

TEACH Services, Inc.
254 Donovan Road
Brushton, NY 12916

info@TEACHServices.com

or you may call us at:

518/358-3494

Produced in partnership with
LNFBooks.com

www.ingramcontent.com/pod-product-compliance
Lightning Source LLC
Chambersburg PA
CBHW070538170426
43200CB00011B/2468